A Day in M

C000143434

Presented by
Aron Bennett

chipmunkapublishing
the mental health publisher

Published by
Chipmunkapublishing
United Kingdom

http://www.chipmunkapublishing.com

Copyright © 2016 Aron Bennett

ISBN   978-1-78382-316-1

Acknowledgements

I would like to express my sincere thanks to all the contributors who made this book possible. Thank you to my parents, who have been so supportive over the years, disputing the contumelious yet brilliant maxim that is the first line of Larkin's infamous poem, 'This Be The Verse'. I forgive you for any hint of 'vicarious acquisition'. Thank you to my only brother, IT whiz kid (or *geek*), for the website I am sure he will build, should the letterpress-bound pages of this manuscript prove successful. Thank you to Clarissa Hopkins for the wonderful editing of all these entries, and thank you to Sanchita Islam for her inspired artwork which forms the main image on the front cover. Thanks to Ross Harrison who generated a platform in which our fine contributors could submit their material. And finally, thanks to Keira Bartlett for not only coming up with the title for this project but for helping compile, organise and even source some of our writers. Thanks also to the charities BEAT and OCD Action, who helped to provide and suggest great writers.

Without all of you, I know this book would not have been possible.

Aron Bennett

Introduction

A Day in My Head? Could there be a more aptly chosen title to describe a diary of this kind. Men and women, ranging in age and ethnicity from around the world, all writing, recording, making public what it is to live and love with mental illness. The stories you will read in this book are both remarkable and yet surprisingly common place all at the very same time. It is a contradiction peculiar only to those experiencing life through a prism; the goggles that fix themselves tightly around the eyes and that fasten often painfully via a long cord of sinew around the temples. Under these conditions, it is no wonder that mundane life events may so readily and easily become transmogrified.

Yet these contributors share one universal truth. A truth that connects them all in the most hermetic way imaginable. A truth that pierces like a hunting spear, the advent of which spans back to early civilization. And the one resounding message: without compassion and understanding we cannot progress. Whether it be debates within our own NHS, pushing the agenda even further for 'parity of esteem', or campaigners in Saudi Arabia fighting for women's rights and gender equality, so as to reduce, amongst other things, female suicide; without compassion and awareness we remain lost and alone. We remain vulnerable, stuck with our own thoughts for company.

The day is May 16th. An ordinary day for many; for some, a day that would change the course of their lives irrevocably. For contributors based here in the UK, this was the start of National Mental Health Awareness Week. People across the Isle - indeed across the whole world - aside from the difficult task of simply surviving, spent any extra energy they had creatively going about generating awareness. For 89 people this involved candidly and courageously writing about their day, about their lives, their experiences, the stigma they face, the isolation and the vulnerability. They wrote about a day in their own heads.

The idea behind the book is simple: the more we talk, the less we have to feel alone. When it comes to mental health, the media is littered with inaccuracies, as well as the occasional vilifying commentary. Under these conditions, it is no wonder so many choose to keep their inner worlds to themselves. This book attempts to lift the lid on shame, and to speak to the many people out there who know or love someone living with mental illness. And to those writing, this book is a chance to bare their souls; to give you, the reader, the transom-like opportunity to peer into the secret life of a person living with disability and adversity. It is a chance to generate the compassion and understanding we all need and deserve ...

From Qatar to Pakistan, Japan, Canada, America, Europe and South Africa, the following stories are all authentic accounts. Some have chosen to write under a pseudonym and others have kept their own names. We have respected their right to privacy. The ages and locations all remain largely accurate.

And so, with a joy in language and in remarkably lyrical prose, I present to you our 89 contributors, each providing a counterweight to those who might have skimmed the topic of mental illness and found it to be vitiating and blackish. And, in its place, offering light.

The below testimony from one of our hundred contributors perhaps sums up what it means to each and every one of us the best:

Name: Sarah Fader
Age: 36
Location: New York City, United States
Condition: Panic Disorder
Profession: CEO of *Stigma Fighters*

"Today my heart opened for the first time in years. There's a secret part of me that I don't reveal to anyone ever. I have been burned, I have been rejected, and it has sent me spiraling into a deep dark hole of depression. Being misunderstood is something I am used to. Today changed all that. You heard me. You felt me. You listened and you did not judge. I will always love you for that. Whether you are 5000 miles away from me or I am embracing you, I know you get me and I get you. And that ... that is love. You changed my life for the better. You brought me out of the darkness and the light shone on my face. Thank you. Thank you for seeing me, my dark, my light, and all of me. I see you. I will always see you. You. Me. All of it."

Ab uno disce omnes. From one, learn all. Today, we learn what it is like for over four hundred and fifty million across the world to forever be present inside of one's own head ...

A New Frontier

Like the infamous *voyage au centre de la terre*, in which protagonist Otto Lidenbrock journeys to the centre of the earth, the mental topography of the everyday 'sufferer' – do we even have the right word here? – remains largely uncharted. It is an untapped terrain. But what does the journey look like? What untold terrors lie beneath the surface ... inside our heads?

Name: Caitlin Hancocks
Age: 20
Condition: Anorexia
Location: Cape Town, Africa do Sul

A day in my head does not consist of hours, minutes and seconds. Those are not the numbers that wrestle with my thoughts. Instead, the numbers are that of calories, kilograms, quantities of consumption and weights of portions.

I wake up to hunger. I fall asleep to hunger. I am starved, yet my body doesn't reveal it. Nobody can see the desperation in my eyes when I glimpse at the snacks at work. Nobody hears my stomach growl until I decide it deserves some food. Nobody sees the thief, the one who rummages through drawers and counts items, hoping the owner will not notice the health bar missing from her stash.

My day is hunger personified. It is not merely physical hunger; the empty hole in my belly. It is also emotional hunger – for love, acceptance, closure, understanding, sympathy, affirmation, support and security. My heart is empty, too.

Along with this hunger are three keys to my day: Anxiety, depression and self-destruction. Anxiety is the quiet shower of absolute fear that drowns me when I appear vulnerable. It opens itself onto me, and pours until my lungs are filled. I cannot breathe, I cannot talk, I cannot think. When it comes it grabs hold of both the mental and physical, and does not stop until both have drowned in the fear. What might this fear be, others may think. This fear is simpler than it seems. It is the fear of everything, everything that could possibly go wrong in any given situation, all at once. Like an ocean it lands on me with all its weight, and that is why I drown.

Depression is the polar opposite to my anxiety. Where anxiety makes me nervous about tasks for the day, depression convinces me that it doesn't even matter. Where anxiety makes me overcompensate and overwork myself, depression paralyses me, debilitating any attempt at progress. It, too, is heavy. Like a mountain it rests on my weak body, and the more I try to shake it, the more it crushes me.

The perfect combination of my anxiety and depression moulds my last key very carefully. They join together to produce the hatred for myself embedded deep within. The internal hatred festers daily. When I feel the anxiety rise, it starts to whisper how pathetic and useless I am, with no hope of success. Then it shouts that I need to work harder, do better. When attempting to do something positive, my depression reminds me that there is no point to my life, I am only wasting space and that I will fail, regardless of my efforts, so why even try. Instead, sit and do nothing other than contemplate my sad existence.

The combination of these – the desperation to be perfect and the demotivation to try for fear of failing – is what stirs the self-destructive thoughts. Anxiety screams at depression, and I purge after binging. Depression cries to anxiety, and leaves a long deep scratch on my skin.

My eating disorder is the face of it all, the perfect product of the cycle of destruction. It fronts for the rest of my disorders. My head may be mine but my mind is not my own. It is only the nest that holds the mess. The modes live together there, and they are in control. They are what you see when you look at me. I don't think they even know Caitlin exists.

Cutting, scratching, binging, starving, purging, drugs, abuse, isolation, pulling out hair. These are the products of two very meek sounding words. They are the contents of my day. The world outside hasn't even featured in my day yet by the time my keys unlock my mind for the new day, when the numbers start and the playlist runs on a loop, all day, every day, in my head.

Name: Sophia Fedorowicz
Age: 27
Condition: Depression
Location: Stoke-on-Trent, United Kingdom

Today I'm so tired my eyelids are concrete. When the show is over, when the crashing crescendo of the weekend has faded and I'm left all alone, that's when it becomes difficult to breathe. The inside of my head is full of cotton wool and no one single clear thought is discernible. I'm wading through a thick, grey, putrid sludge and making no progress. I stayed in bed today. I lay in bed all day. My vacant eyes tracing the edges of the screen I was staring at. I couldn't even concentrate on the colours of the

A Day in My Head

moving images, the sounds of the voices, it was all garbage, utter life-destroying garbage, sucking my soul out through my nose. I only put it on because if someone sees me, they'll just think I'm watching television. Not staring at the wall for eleven hours and waiting for sleep, as if it were death.

Today has not been my day. I almost anticipated the low feelings because of the consistent high feelings over the weekend. What goes up must come down. It must come crashing down to earth in a burning, blinding ball of perfect misfigured humanity. To be human is to be flawed and contradictory. Graceful yet graceless.

I have to pick my battles and today is a graceless kind of day; I can't win this one and telling myself that I should win only reinforces feelings of failure. I can let myself be vacant. Just for today. Accept the things I cannot change.

From the outside, to look at me it may seem like I have given up, but inside I am fighting. I am plotting and planning, I am digging and clawing my way out of the black hole I have tripped and fallen into. Tomorrow I will use all the tools I have gathered and refined in group and I will get out of this hole. I will drag myself, crying and wounded, across the floor, covered in dirt towards the light. Tomorrow will be a better day. Tomorrow I will be graceful.

Name: Zarayna Marie
Age: 26
Condition: Depression, Anxiety, Obsessive Compulsive Disorder
Location: London, United Kingdom

I woke up this morning and there they were again; he was sitting on my head and she was sitting on my chest. I am talking about my two best friends, depression and anxiety.

Anxiety is always red and depression is always blue. And I see them when I look in the mirror, so now I am purple, I move around with a purple haze, and not in a good way like Prince with Purple Rain. In a really bad way, like the cloud that follows you everywhere you go, when people walk past you they do a double take and point and stare, "She's mental you know, look at her purple haze. She's a basket case."

How is it possible to feel completely numb, yet feel every single bit of pain in the world? Yesterday was exhausting enough, I can't do this anymore, I can't take one more day of this.

And all I can think is please, please, please don't make me do this again. And this is all before I have even got out of bed.

What am I getting out of bed for anyway? It's not as if I am going to do anything, or if I am going to make a difference, or if I am going to amount to anything anyway! This is depression talking – "Stay in bed with me, I'll keep you company, I'll hold you close and keep you safe and be your friend. That's what you are meant to do, stay and be with me." Then after staring at the ceiling I pull the duvet over my head because I know exactly what's coming next.

I can feel it building up and up and up, here she comes, here comes Anxiety! Bam! Like someone punching me in the face, full blown panic attack. I can't breathe, I AM GOING TO DIE! Oh My God. 10 minutes ago I prayed for death and now he's here. I am having a heart attack. OH MY GOD. OH MY GOD. BREATHE. JUST BREATHE. JUST BREATHE! How can I breathe? My heart is trying to break through my chest, not just a little flutter, I can actually see my whole body convulsing. I'm getting dizzy, I'm about to pass out, it's hot, oh my God it's hot, sweating. Just Breathe! In through the nose, out through the mouth, in through the nose out through the mouth. Remember what you learnt in CBT, do your breathing exercises. Oh no, there goes the blood draining from the muscles in my stomach. I'm going to be sick. Quick run to the bathroom, but there is no feeling in your legs during an anxiety attack. I'm now running to the bathroom on jelly. And then nothing.

Then he comes back. "Well you're out of bed now, you may as well spend the day with me." Here we go again, him sitting on my head and her wrapped around my chest. Another day with Anxiety and Depression!

Name: Professor David Veale FRcPsych, FBPsS, MPhil, BSc, MD
Profession: Consultant Psychiatrist in Cognitive Behaviour Therapy
Operating From: The South London and Maudsley NHS Foundation
Trust and The Priory Hospital North London

I would hate to have even an hour living in my head. It would drive me mad. Living in your head is a major health issue as bad as smoking. It is often ignored but cuts across many mental health problems. If you live in your head, then you get all the information about yourself and others from your inner world and the ghosts from the past. Thus, if you feel anxious then there must be a threat. If you think you are bad then it must be true. If an image tells you that you look disgusting, then that is how you appear to others. If you hear voices then it will have come from your own thoughts.

A Day in My Head

One strategy in cognitive behaviour therapy is therefore to help an individual refocus on the external world, what you can see, what you can hear, what you can smell, and doing it without judging or comparing yourself. This is of course a difficult task because our minds are designed to keep us safe and to attend to threat. In many mental disorders a part of your inner world has become the threat. Therefore, some scientists argue that therapists are trying to tackle the problem too late. If one can, it is better to try to update any memories of bad experiences that are still emotionally linked to the present. In addition it's helpful to have a good understanding of what the problem is and how you may be misinterpreting the thought or images. It's still important to act against how you feel and to approach difficulties rather than avoid them. The goal must be to get out of one's head, unless you are trying to be creative or solve actual problems or reflect on your behaviour to help you to change – though even then it would be for just a limited period ...

"Sleep, those little slices of death"

Sleep complications are the bane of most people's lives and are a common symptom of mental illness, spanning the spectrum of conditions touched on in this book. Insomnia and other chronic sleep disorders both increase the risk of and even directly contribute to a plethora of psychiatric conditions. And, whether a symptom or a cause, sleep problems have an undoubtedly large impact, experientially, as some of our contributors can testify.

Name: KB
Age: 28
Condition: Anxiety, Depression
Location: Norwich, United Kingdom

It's 1.30am and I awake after being asleep for just short of three hours, mind racing, I lie in bed using mindfulness techniques in an attempt to block out the tinnitus ringing in my ears, hoping to calm my mind enough to fall asleep again. It seems to work for a short period but then I find myself waking again at 4am. My internal dialogue starts to chatter and question whether I'd actually fallen asleep again, whether the same will happen tomorrow night, what if I can't function properly during the day, what if I'm heading back to the same place I found myself in last year.

To most, this kind of sleepless night won't sound like a big deal - it happens to all of us from time to time. But to me, it's a reminder of a dark period of my life last year in which, at my worst, caused no sleep for three nights straight, and the nights I did manage to fall asleep I'd wake every couple of hours without fail. The less I slept the more negatively affected my mental state in the day time became; I was stuck in a horrible cycle of no sleep, increasingly anxiety filled days, and an overwhelming sense of dread and fear.

I believed I was going insane or had some horrible incurable disease that no doctor had managed to diagnose. I needed an answer as to why I was feeling this way, almost hoping it was some terrible disease as I would, at least, have an explanation. I searched the internet looking for answers to my symptoms (bad idea), and during the space of around three months had multiple blood tests, brain scans, hearing test, CT scans, visited multiple specialists and four different GPs. All results came back clear.

A Day in My Head

But I knew something wasn't right and yet no one could find anything wrong, which only served to magnify my symptoms. The list is probably long enough to fill this entire entry, so I've highlighted the main ones:

Headaches
Tinnitus
Feeling of being spaced out/disconnected
Shaking/twitching
Clumsiness
Forgetfulness
Sensitive to noises/music
Paranoia
Butterflies in stomach
Tingling limbs and face
Insomnia
Aching
Panic attacks
Overwhelming feelings of dread/fear for no reason
Strange unsettling thoughts
Fear of losing control
Racing thoughts
Hypochondria

I was experiencing a serious episode of mixed anxiety and depression. But I didn't have any reason for this to happen to me. I have a good life, solid job, caring family/girlfriend, and lots to look forward to, but for reasons unknown still to this day I became trapped in my mind. For the ensuing months I truly believed I was broken and would never feel well again, dropping almost two stone in weight and signed off from work (I'd not had a sick day in over five years prior to this episode).

Despite being absolutely terrified about what was happening, deep down part of me knew I didn't want to feel this way. I had too much to lose to just give in and accept this was me from now on. I started reading about anxiety, reading about other people's experiences, practicing mindful meditation, and with the support of my family I started to realise I wasn't alone, and although this didn't stop the symptoms it did start to reduce the fear I had about them.

Back to today ...

I get out of bed and ready for work with the "what if's" from the night before still fresh in my mind, I remind myself how far I've come since last year, most of the time I feel well and from the outside looking in you'd probably think nothing had happened.

13

Little things throughout my day act as reminders: the ringing in my ears, forgetting where I put my keys, headaches, tiredness, what did the neighbour think of me after I said good morning. Setting off the internal chatter. Before last summer I would have thought nothing of these tiny everyday events, now they're internal battles with my own mind and reminders that I'm still very raw from last summer.

I finish the evening by instructing a Tae Kwon Do class, which helps to switch my mind off for at least an hour. A small victory, proving to myself that I'm not broken, a step closer to full acceptance, and a reminder that I can get through even the darkest periods.

Name: Nicole L
Age: 18
Condition: Social Anxiety Disorder, Generalised Anxiety Disorder, Panic Disorder, Obsessive Compulsive Disorder
Location: Toronto, Canada

The only time I am at peace with myself is when I'm asleep. Once I wake I'm filled with the terrible thoughts again. The nightmares from the night before. All of my life's problems. All of the mistakes I've made in my life. In my mind there is no peace – there is only fear and sadness.

Anxiety isn't something that comes and goes for me. It is a constant that only changes in respect of what specifically is *on* my mind, whether it's the intrusive thoughts of the people I care about dying; the fear of screwing up on my latest school project; the fear of being judged by everyone around me; the fear of having a panic attack so intense I feel like I'm experiencing an inner-earthquake; they all have a role to play in my anxiety. The manifestation is merely a product of *time*.

My morning starts, as usual, with recounting the horrible thoughts I had the night before. Most of the time it's death or violence of some kind, but sometimes there is some horrible sexual aspect to it. These thoughts build up all day and by night time I am genuinely wondering what is going to happen to me. Following this, I stick rigidly to my routine of getting dressed, brushing my hair and having breakfast before heading off to another stressful day at school. Though school is hard for most, I don't have much difficulty with it – it's only my head that makes it difficult. My concentration may be diminished if something horrible happened the night before, which would lead me to be distracted by anxiety. School, at many times, *causes* some of the anxiety. Presenting in front of everyone sitting at their seats, for example, makes me feel like I have a spotlight over me. Sometimes there are so many projects and tests going on, all leading to exams, that there never seems to be a break. This internal anxiety and

A Day in My Head

stress may build up inside my body until I am experiencing a full blown panic attack. My heart is racing, I'm sweating, my whole body feels like the inside of a volcano, I'm shaking like a volcano, my world is spinning, my chest feels like a boulder has landed on it. My body may express its anxiety this way. It may also cause my entire body to feel like it's covered in mud, creating the urge to wash my hands over and over again. This feeling never goes until my anxiety and stress is over.

My anxiety levels fluctuate. Today I consider to be a good day. Other days I want to lock myself in a room and cry out all the pain and suffering. Fear and anxiety is something I live with. It has moulded me to see a different side to the world, one in which our minds are our own worst enemies. But it has also taught me that there are others like me. There are ways to make myself better. Anxiety doesn't have to control my life. Anxiety doesn't have to control anyone's life. It just needs to serve as a reminder that our minds are all different and that, through hard work, our worries may be repositioned suitably to the back of our minds. But for now, I still struggle with generalized and social anxiety disorder, panic disorder, and obsessive-compulsive disorder.

One day soon, I hope more than anything that I will be able to transform these conditions, these *labels*, into a *strength*.

Name: Laura Nuttal
Age: 26
Condition: Schizoaffective Disorder
Location: Ruskington, United Kingdom

When my alarm screeched at 5am this morning I was already wide awake but desperately needing sleep. Whilst my mental health is currently stable and I am able to function normally, the medication maintaining my wellness leaves me feeling sedated. It also plays havoc with my sleep pattern, meaning I rarely manage to sleep through the night. As I dragged myself out of bed to start the day, my eyes burned and my eyelids felt heavy but I felt positive about the day ahead.

Luckily I was only on shift for two hours this morning. I love being able to work as I hate being financially dependent on my parents at the age of 26 but I never feel good enough. I was recently admitted to an acute psychiatric ward, meaning I was required to take an extended period of sick leave and, whilst my colleagues have been very supportive, I have been told by the 'top dogs' that a re-occurrence of these more severe symptoms could result in my contract being terminated. This has left me even more terrified of my own illness ... of my own mind. I feel as though I have to appear okay even when I'm not feeling well.

15

Today, like other days, I questioned odd sounds and sights, worried that they were actually hallucinations and a sign that I was becoming unwell. That's the thing about Schizoaffective Disorder – it's unpredictable. Today, like other days, I wore a smile and engaged with others so that my 'wellness' was evident for all to see. Today, like other days, I 'lived life', despite desperately wanting to hide under my duvet just hours after leaving the safety of my bed.

I have been trying to be productive recently to prevent me from spending hour upon hour in a half asleep state on the sofa (whilst my mind and body often want to do this, I find myself feeling low and guilty when I do). I ended up going to the local garden centre with my sister and buying far too many plants to revamp the garden with. The afternoon flew past and I felt quite proud of the finished result. It was surprisingly therapeutic and, whilst focussing on the repetitive motions of digging and planting, my mind felt at peace.

My mood does tend to drop slightly in the evening and it has today. It's almost as though the effort I have put in to resisting negative thoughts and behaviours becomes a little too tiring and anxieties start to creep and crawl within me, making me feel sick and my muscles feel tense. Whilst I can usually distract myself from these feelings by watching television or practising mindfulness, tonight is proving a little more challenging. I am not experiencing any significant life stresses that the average person doesn't face from time to time, but I do feel as though I am not as capable and as strong as others. If I'm honest, I feel guilty for feeling that way - almost as though I am making myself out to be some sort of vulnerable victim. I'm not – I know that I am capable and strong deep down … I just have to try and remind myself of that on a regular basis. I think it's more about self-esteem than anything evidential.

It's now 10:30pm. I am writing this in my pyjamas with my springer spaniel curled up beside me, his presence as comforting as ever. I have managed another day and, all-in-all, it has been a good'un! Now all that is left for me to do is take my pills and try and get some sleep. I always try and make sure to tell myself that tomorrow will be okay despite how much I might disbelieve it at times. I refuse to let mental illness steal hope from my life.

Name: Kathryn Hockey
Age: 49
Condition: Depression
Location: Vejer de la Frontera, Spain

I am in celebratory mode, having just had a three stage oral vaccine, consisting of a sugared pill, a spray and a sticky mouthwash; before that I

A Day in My Head

was on a beach listening to my dad discuss my cousin's house extension and property portfolio, and before that I'd managed to fend off an amorous advance from Noam Chomsky.

Ah-ha, lying in my diary – well not entirely; I was chronicling my series of early morning dreams, that's why I'm feeling celebratory, the dreams mean that I got back to sleep after waking too early in the dark again with the heart-sink feeling that it was going to be another sandy-eyed, confusing day of fatigue and resentment for insomnia. But I did it. I got back to sleep before the whirring, obsessive mind hooked into wakefulness.

My best trick for sleep is simple but I often forget it, or more accurately I get trapped in the fantasy replay my mind projectionist offers as "entertainment" which is actually self sabotage, and as toxic as worry in its ability to induce sleeplessness. I managed to all but give up worry some time ago but the 'fantasyland' habit is harder to kick.

So the off switch: Breathe in. Breathe out. Sometimes it's so hard to focus on breathing that I lie in bed for hours half asleep with a warped daydream replaying in my head, over and over. But other times, if I can just concentrate on 'breathe in, breathe out' for long enough I am delivered into sweet, elusive, mysterious sleep.

The eight o'clock bells are ringing, I made six hours. Still sleepy but refreshed.

The 11.30 bells have just rung. I'm on the roof, there's jazz playing in the paper workshop below. The birds are chirping and swooping, flapping and courting and the jumble of village below me ends before the softly undulating countryside which sweeps out to the distant hazy mountains. Even as I register contentment, the buzz of anxiety whirs in my middle and my eyes become tired in the glare of the sun.

It's a truly beautiful day, all I need to do is remember to concentrate on the positive and the breathing.

6pm and I'm back on the roof watching the swallows dive in joyful squadrons, there's a half moon high in the blue sky, a gentle breeze and a lone gliding vulture. I'm recuperating from a considerable period of stress, culminating last week in the success of a crowd funding campaign to raise money to self-publish a picture book for adults about depression and hope.

I drew on my experience of depression to make the illustrations for my collaborator's poem, an intense process which took about nine months of

17

imagining, externalising and depicting my demons as well as my methods for coping with them. Then I had to make it all public. I did have misgivings about the last part but it seems that the work has given other people permission to open up about their own psychological battles and they have given it a warm and humbling reception.

Promotion, publicity and fundraising are not my favourite tasks and my collaborator assured me that he would bear the brunt of that part of the book launch, but for various reasons he went away and it was left to me. I felt let down and abandoned and got quite upset and angry but I carried on. Because I had managed to externalise my demons in the illustrations, and let out my emotions by ranting to a couple of sympathetic friends, and doing boxing training, those demons didn't take me down into the dark again.

The stress has definitely impacted my physical health so it's now vital that I concentrate my efforts on relaxation, positive thinking and mindful self-care. There are many, many more
beautiful days to come. Breathe.

The Black Dawg – an illustrated poem about Depression and Hope will be available 30th September 2016

Name: Cathy Clarke
Age: 47
Condition: Obsessive Compulsive Disorder
Location: Greater Manchester, United Kingdom

The alarm reverberates in my ear like a Tibetan gong. Momentarily, I feel the warmth of the sun seeping through my window and onto my crumpled face, crease marked by my pillow. It feels like nourishment, and for a few seconds I am happy, as I hear my son laughing in his room whilst the kittens cavort on his bed and dodge his tickling hands. However, this moment of calm, this almost meditative state, is lost when I catch a glimpse of my dishevelled pyjamas on the radiator, the pain medication on my bedside table and when I remember what an awful night's sleep I have just had.

Last night my OCD thoughts were like a swirling vortex of medical definitions. Every twinge in my body caused me to Google my symptoms and I spent hours reading through complicated medical journals and looking at gruesome images of internal organs riddled with cancer. Most people briefly entertain the fact that they might be seriously ill at some point in their lives, but they don't spend days researching conditions or examining their bodies for signs of illness. I have had cancer in two separate places, but for years I imagined the worst, even when I was free

A Day in My Head

of the malignancy. It was almost a relief to be diagnosed because, at least for a short time, I was reassured that the doctors had everything under control and I trusted their opinion. That only lasted for a few weeks. Then the fear that they had missed a tumour or that a rogue cell had travelled to my kidneys, my brain or my bones festered in my mind and I began to Google again, every tiny twinge, every little mole, every ache and creak, everything. By the time the morning comes I am exhausted. I have read for hours, feel really agitated and this does not bode well for my other OCD symptoms because sleep deprivation only makes them worse.

Suddenly the thought of getting out of bed and beginning my morning routine seems insurmountable. As I lie there, I dwell too long on the fact that I had to leave my teaching career after having cancer. The disease gave me B12 deficiency and super charged my OCD. My OCD at work led me to become obsessed by data. It gnawed away at me and was all I could think about. It's not even 7am and my brain is so overloaded by fear and self-loathing for having to leave a job I loved with a passion, that I have not noticed that I'm in an OCD loop of thought. I'm going to be late.

Imagine for a moment what it is like to be in the eye of a storm. Hurricanes have a vortex, a centre point where everything is calm that calm is how I feel when I wake, but move slightly left or right and you are hit by twisted gusts of wind carrying debris that has been ripped brutally from the land. Being hit by the debris is unavoidable; you are not in control any more. The swirling mass of detritus leaves you frightened and disorientated and you can't steer your way clear of the dangers; you are not going to survive this horrific experience. You flail your limbs in random directions trying to steady yourself but you are just met with more flying projectiles. Those projectiles are OCD thoughts. Once in an OCD loop (Pure O in my case), you cannot wrench your mind free. It takes goliath strength and determination to re-focus your thoughts away from the ones that frighten you and back into a composed frame of mind. However, all too often, by the time that you manage to do this, you are late for whatever appointment you have that day. Usually by this stage, I have been sitting on the edge of my bed for 30 minutes lost in thought, saved only by a shout from my husband saying goodbye.

I haven't even left my bedroom yet and I feel thoroughly lost. Tiredness overwhelms me. I want the sunlight back in my life but I'm continually caught in a never ending storm; a vicious OCD loop. The loop stops me writing because I can't concentrate and it fills me with self-doubt and dread. My life is restricted, frightening and unlived because of OCD.

You can follow Cathy Clarke on Twitter @caughtinanocdloop.com

De Omnius Dubitandum

De Omnius Dubitandum or, in English, *All is to be doubted*. Most famously applied by Christopher Hitchens in his *Letters to a Young Contrarian,* in which the examinate polemicist urges readers to do what they must to combat atrophy and routine. Though for those living with mental illness, often conceding this imperative is much easier said than done. Doubt and routine, for this group, are perhaps in every sense contrapositive. For most of our contributors, All is certainly doubted. And yet the atrophy and routine remains stiflingly and viciously ever-present ...

Name: Tuesday Turner
Age: 26
Condition: Obsessive Compulsive Disorder, Depression
Location: Bridgend, Mid Glamorgan, United Kingdom

Another Day with the Bleach Bottle ...

Not that it's anything out of the ordinary of course, it's just that for the past few days my hands have started to bleed again, becoming burnt and swollen. It's expected though, using neat bleach daily on everything throughout my home from the light switches to the insides of my shoes is bound to do some damage. And although it inevitably causes me some pain as my already raw fingers are routinely exposed to bleach and other cleaning chemicals, I don't have the option of wearing rubber gloves to protect my skin because, even amidst the discomfort, my OCD still gets some satisfaction knowing that my hands will be germ free.

Right now, having finished work for the day, contamination is at its peak. I've been at the office, used a keyboard, sat on a chair, touched handles, people have brushed past me, touched me, and, worst of all, someone had the flu and actually did the unthinkable by sneezing near me! I did the usual freaking out in my own subtle way of covering my nose with my hand so as not to breathe in the germs and casually moved away from the vicinity. I made my way over to the office kitchen to wash my hands, aware that I hadn't touched anything since the last time I'd washed them but still fearing that germs may have somehow infected me through that person's sneeze and, other than take a shower, washing my hands was the best I could do to satisfy the OCD monster whilst I was at work.

A Day in My Head

My routines limit contamination whilst I'm at the office, such as sitting on paper rather than allowing my clothes to touch the germs on the seat, or opening doors with tissue paper. The keyboard is one of the worst for me though. I apply just a thin coating of bleach to the buttons, monitor, mouse and desk area around every hour to keep germs at a minimum, so long as nobody notices. Although people I work alongside have realised I'm overly clean, that's as far as anybody's knowledge goes on the topic. You see, I tend to keep my contamination anxieties quiet for numerous reasons - embarrassment and hostility from others - but largely because I find it so exhausting explaining to someone who has absolutely no understanding of how difficult it was for me to leave my confined, bleach bubble of a home that morning, that by the time I have tried to educate them they still define it as something funny, quirky and to be taken lightly. I'm speaking from experience here. For example, I once had one person stick their finger in their mouth and wipe their spit across my arm after I tried to explain why I don't hug people, and another tell me how "stupid" my fears of germs and contamination were. Therefore, for the sake of not having to punch anybody for making such ignorant and uninformed comments, I simply stay quiet and try to raise awareness through bigger and better means, largely mental health charities and volunteer work.

I don't just suffer with OCD though. As with many sufferers, it's combined with depression, anxiety and intrusive thoughts, a combination which can only be described as the most soul crushing misery that can take over your mind and body, and all that you can do is believe that it will pass. I've done the crying, screaming, self-harming, locking myself away, aggression and even a suicide attempt when I was 19, but now, at the age of 26, a new combination of medications seem to be helping me think more clearly and see a less hopeless future. Although the OCD is still running the show, my determination to work and travel the world are the only factors that allow me to take a little bit of control back because these things make me feel the wonder of actual happiness, something I'm well overdue and plan to get a lot of in the future.

Name: Jane Estry
Age: 29
Condition: Borderline Personality Disorder, Eating Disorder
Location: Huddersfield, United Kingdom

Today started like most others, a forty minute snooze session, a bite on the toes from the cat and a hangover – even though I hadn't actually drunk last night. As I lay in bed I practiced my CBT techniques and visualised myself getting up, having a shower, using my face wash, getting up, using my face wash, having a shower, using my face wash, getting up, face, shower, wash.... Try as I might, I can never successfully list more than three details without having to repeat myself. Cognitive chaos always ensues before my first drink (non-alcoholic, might I add).

Mondays, being particularly depressing, further delayed my bed-exodus so I lolled there for a further seventeen minutes ingesting a load of shite on Facebook and the like. This meant that I had around eight minutes to get ready; personal target: thirty. The first thing I did when I got up was remove everything from my person, – everything – hair grips, bobbles, earrings, nail varnish, sleep from my eyes ... then I weighed myself and hoped that somehow overnight I'd managed to achieve my desired weight loss. When my halcyon weight goal didn't materialise I moved the scales round four more times in some kind of weird weight loss tessellation wish and settled on the lowest number.

After having a 90 second shower in which I managed to successfully shave my armpits and clean my teeth simultaneously, I started to come round slightly. In what can only be described as a sordid laundry fumble, I seized a crumpled selection of semi appropriate work wear (from my floor) and examined it for creases. I'm not sure why I do this because I haven't actually ironed anything since the late 1990s.

Slimming World dictates that I *must* have breakfast, even though the thought of it makes me feel like ripping my tongue out and throwing it at the wall, so I made my warm lemon water, courtesy of Women's Health Mag circa 2009, and ate four spoonful's of low-fat plain yoghurt, with great disdain. Once in the car and on my way to work I felt my mood lift – at exactly the same point as I always do – Cocking Crow Stone. I managed to apply my make up and do my hair in situ, which was both dangerous and an accomplishment.

Work was exceptionally busy today as I rammed all of my appointments into two days. Today was the type of day where I felt compassionate, empathetic and kind when listening to people's job woes. Sometimes I want to fucking stab them. At lunch I had a small wholemeal ham sandwich with a piece of fruit and four seafood sticks. I ate it at my desk so as to avoid both small talk and the tuck shop goodies, but mainly the small talk. My final appointment was a no show which, publicly, I pretended to be exasperated by, but secretly I was delighted as I was able to leave early and beat the school traffic.

The long journey into work is a blessing as I am able to focus on improving my mood and that heavy hangover feeling dissipates; however,

A Day in My Head

the journey home is an actual curse. It gives me time to ruminate, examine every problem in its extreme minutia, and I find myself having imaginary conversations or full blown rows. I worked myself up so much today that I was ready to leave *darling boyfriend* for not pulling his weight in the house. When I got home he'd started redecorating the hall so I reversed my silent seethe, gave him a kiss and felt like a right arsehole.

Seeing as I was so hungry (calorie app tracker told me I was well below my daily limit) I made an earlyish tea of minced meat pizza – sounds vile but is actually a household favourite. We watched *Dinner Date* whilst eating and slagged off our colleagues. *Darling Boyfriend* suggested going for an evening cycle but I really couldn't be arsed so I made up some lame excuse about having a load of work to do and a two minute minor argument ensued surrounding the importance of not restricting food but upping exercise instead. Really wish I was as motivated as he is.

We went up to bed at about ten thirty and watched the beginning of a war film which prompted another mini row - as if sleep isn't hard enough for me without the cacophony of machine guns and murder. With the TV off, *Darling Boyfriend* immediately drifted off into a blissful slumber whilst I wondered what it would be like to be able to mentally unwind so quickly, even for just one night.

Name: Edward Boylett
Age: 21
Condition: Anxiety, Panic Disorder
Location: Cardiff, United Kingdom

DAILY REMINDER:

"All we need is daylight" - Gustav Wood, Young Guns

Hello,

Today a slow morning follows a heavily wakeful night, in which I struggled to overcome the tussles and turns and the bizarrely sauna-like nature of my bedroom. The morning drags as my daily argument ensues with myself, over the pathetic feeling of how long it takes me to mentally prepare to open the front door, even though I have to be somewhere in less than half an hour. Eventually, once I've made it out the door, I put on my headphones and attempt some calming music, another staple of my daily routine.

I make it into the city centre, and my 12pm meeting passes by with ease and is complimented by the offer of a job interview for tomorrow. I make my way to a coffee shop, intent on applying for more jobs and looking up local agencies to apply to. I have my usual order and sit in my usual seat, as I have become somewhat of a regular now. I survey the shop and look at those around; I am the only person sitting alone. My head decides to give me a relatively polite kick and reminder that this is my decision, but I refrain from actually cursing at myself in public. Things seem to be fine after this, say other than the occasional comment I make to myself. I feel fine. However, this comes to a grinding halt as the internet connection cuts out and a job application I've been working on empties itself upon reloading. Yet again that voice in my head pops up and I find myself frustrated and am suddenly aware that a couple of the members of staff are looking over at me. I reach for my music again and give myself a breather from applications.

This is where I think on the positives: I am not doing as bad as I was just a few weeks ago, when the last days of university were in full swing and I was experiencing panic attacks frequently and couldn't shake the fear of failure from my mind. And I've managed to keep a relatively calm state since finishing. This is when I look to the quote I've put at the top of this entry, a reminder of the words I have tattooed on me: There will always be another day in which something different will happen. I've been to my very worst, and everything I am doing is to avoid ever returning to the way I felt then.

I know I've still got the rest of the day to go, but despite a blip in internet connectivity, today has gone relatively well, and when I finally leave the coffee shop I am feeling relaxed and happy. I am, however, aware of the yawning that I keep trying to hide, and know that my body is trying to tell me it needs more sleep and so, against my better judgement, think I will head for an afternoon nap.

Until next time,

Eddie

Name: Matt
Age: 44
Condition: Dissociation, Anxiety, Post Traumatic Stress Disorder, Survivor of Childhood Sexual Abuse
Location: Pennsylvania, United States
Profession: Blogger, Advocate and Podcaster for Mental Health Awareness

Waking up on this particular day starts out very similarly to most other days. Living with Dissociation, Anxiety, and PTSD is a daily

A Day in My Head

struggle, a battle in my head in which the outcome can go either way.

The day starts with rolling out of bed, after hitting the snooze at least two or three times and trying to get that last minute or two remaining in the safe confines of my room. The world doesn't seem quite so imposing when I'm home. I can be myself, I can control my surroundings, it's one of the few safe places where I can just be me.

Getting to work, the day is filled with conference calls, project managers who want to know how my part of their project is going, and a supervisor who, although he doesn't micro manage very often, still waits in the wings to drop a bombshell of a "hurry up and do this yesterday" nature. The day is further filled with Dissociating when a stressful situation takes over because a piece of equipment is broken and they need an engineer to fix it ASAP.

Most of the time, my mind will take over and take me away temporarily, removing me from the stress as best it can. I'll trace the corners of the walls in my cube or try and ground myself in my chair by placing my feet firmly on the floor. I might also focus on the computer clock for a couple of minutes and watch the time tick so I'm not worried about what's potentially coming when I pick up that phone.

As the minutes tick away towards the end of the day, I can see a light at the end of the tunnel. "Just get through this last hour, these last few minutes. I hope something doesn't go sideways before I'm ready to walk out the door."

Driving home, I'm thinking of how boring my evening will be if my youngest son is at his mom's for the night or my older two kids aren't stopping by. What will my night be filled with? Watching TV perhaps, maybe just read a book, or fall asleep on the couch. What an exciting life I lead.

I could go for a walk or a bike ride. I do enjoy those things, but that only lasts a short time, and it could rain so maybe I just shouldn't bother. Are there some friends online I could chat with tonight? Well I see some active on Twitter and Facebook, but they are probably busy and I shouldn't interrupt. I mean, after all, who am I to butt into their conversation? There aren't any active chats tonight, it's a Thursday evening so there goes that idea.

Maybe I'll do some writing – yes, that's a great idea! I'll write about my last therapy session, the latest problems with my mother, how my son came home the other day and said somebody was picking on him. I could write about why Anxiety just sucks and rules my life so much. I mean, after all, that's what it feels like.

I worry about what could or might happen in any given situation and make sure that I over analyse every possible situation so I'm prepared for the worst. All the while, I haven't yet grasped that preparing for the worst doesn't allow me to enjoy the moment and live life to its fullest.

So I do some writing, listen to some music, play my bass to try to pass the time. It's fulfilling for a while and I've managed to get through the day and now it's time for bed.

How long will I be up – will my mind shut off? It's running at the speed of light to the point that even the Millennium Falcon couldn't possibly keep up.

Put on your ambient sounds, play some quiet music and just lay there.... Sleep will come eventually. Just in time to wake up and start over again.

You can follow Matt @ www.SurvivingMyPast.net

Name: Jade Johnson
Age: 36
Condition: Anxiety Disorder
Location: Norwich, United Kingdom

I woke at 5am today in a panic about my cat.... I'm not even sure why ... but so many possibilities run through my head ...

I've slept ok, which means I'm hopeful for a good day. The weekend has been uneventful and I've felt calm so there's no reason for it not to be. The reality of it being another day and all I have to do takes my breath away.... I want to stay in bed. I need to.

I take my medication. I've been on a low dose of Sertraline since New Year when finally those anxious voices became too much for me ... the forced busyness isn't working anymore. Until later on in my life, I could never admit to how I felt.... I'd rather people

A Day in My Head

thought I was lazy, rude or that I made no effort than that I was anxious.

I have the same routine now. I take my Sertraline and feel like I'm a failure for doing so. If I had a mantra it would be "I'm a failure". I list all my massive failings in my head, all the really big ones, and let myself feel the pain of every single one.

I never wanted to be like this; my anxiety has been my best friend and my worst enemy as long as I can remember. It's always there for me; a constant that I'm actually afraid to be without, yet something that has prevented me from trying so many things and finding joy in so many others. At times it has made me bitter and cruel. My anxiety knows exactly what to say to me to confirm all the things I don't like about myself.

I want to write a list but the head fogs too much.... I'm overwhelmed by thoughts that my house isn't clean enough, my dog didn't get walked enough, I'm not organised enough ... I am just never ... *enough.*

When I pick my son up from pre-school there are things I've forgotten, events and paperwork to add to my list of today's failures. This gives me another chance to list all my major failures and feel that pain again ... right across my chest and in my heart. I've skipped my lunch so I feel smug about that.... I've missed another meal no one knows about ... but the guilt hits me ... I have made promises that I would eat ... and the list of failures comes out again.

I try really hard to function for my kids. Some days it's harder; today is one of those. I'm cooking dinner and a thought pops into my head: "maybe I'll kill myself", like "maybe I will have a cuppa". It's not the first time I've thought this today but it's louder and more intense. It makes me laugh as I'm actually petrified of dying.

I go to meditation on a Monday and for an hour I feel clear... but I'm only pretending to accept my feelings and be kind to myself ... really I'm trying to push all my feelings deep, deep down.

When I walk home the noise of all my worries invades my head.... I replay everything from today, every text, every conversation ... and I think to myself what an absolute twat I am.... I cringe at how useless I am.

Today has been awful ... my body aches so much from it all and I desperately want to sleep ... I'm hopeful for a better day tomorrow

... and for a brief moment I feel glad because at least I still have hope.

Name: Hannah Lewis
Age: 22
Condition: Obsessive Compulsive Disorder, Body Dysmorphic Disorder, General Anxiety Disorder, Social Anxiety Disorder, Depression, Transient Psychosis and Borderline Personality Disorder
Location: London, United Kingdom

A day in the life of a persistently panicked, obsessive-compulsive, body-dysmorphic depressive.

1,2,3,4 ...

What time is it? What time did I get to sleep last night? Have I had enough sleep? How am I feeling today? I'm okay. Am I okay? Yeah I think I'm fine. Am I fine?

I'm hungry. I should eat breakfast. Should I eat breakfast? Have I got enough food in? How fat am I today? I'm fat, I should skip breakfast. No, breakfast is the meal of the day. I need energy to do things. Skipping breakfast makes you put on weight. I'll just have some fruit.

I'm sleepy. I need coffee. I should cut out caffeine. What time is it? Do I have enough time to get ready? I better hurry. Oh god I'm behind schedule. I'm not going to have enough time to do my hair. My hair is going to be a mess today. I can't afford to have bad hair.

My skin is horrible. I look gross. I look so frightening. I look like a monster, like a beast. What if a child sees me today? What if I scare them, give them nightmares? I'll have a shower, that'll make me feel better.

2,4,6,8 ...

How long have I been in the shower? I bet I'm behind schedule. I better do my make up as quickly as possible.

Oh! That doesn't look right. I better put more make up on that spot.

Oh! I've put too much make up on that spot. What's the weather like today?

What shall I wear? I can't wear that, I look too fat. I can't wear that, I'll be too hot. I can't wear that, I'll be too cold. What shall I wear?! I have no

A Day in My Head

clothes. I need more clothes. When do I have time to go shopping? I have no money to buy new clothes.

What time is it? Oh no, I'm going to be late. Have I packed my bag correctly? Do I have everything? I've forgotten something.

What time is it? I'm going to be late. I won't be late. It doesn't matter if I'm late. Yes it does, everybody will look at me. Nobody will look at me. Where's the bus? What's he looking at? I knew I shouldn't have worn this today. I need more clothes. I have no money. Where's the bus? Here's the bus. Oh god, there's too many people on this bus. When's the next one? If I wait for the next one I'll definitely be late. Oh! There's no room. Everyone's looking at me. I look awful, don't I? I bet I smell really bad.

No, I can't smell. I had a shower this morning. But this bus is so full! I'm sweating really badly. It's too hot. There are too many people. I need to get off this bus. No, I can't get off here it's too far from university. I'll just wait. I'm halfway there. You can do this.

But it's so hot. I'm sweating so much. Everyone's looking at me. They're laughing at me. I have sweat on my face. The sweat is going to smudge my makeup. I knew I put too much on today. Is my heart beating too fast? Am I going to have a panic attack? Is that number divisible by four?

Is this a panic attack? Am I dying? Should I die? No it's okay, I'll just breathe. Imagine the
waves of the ocean. What time is it? Am I on time? I'll be on time if I hurry to class. No, I can't hurry I'll sweat more.

4, 8, 12, 16 ...

Will I be like this forever? When will I not have to panic all the time? Where's my classroom? I've forgotten. I've remembered. It's this one. Am I late? Everyone's looking at me. No they're not. The class hasn't even started. Am I going to pass this class? I'm going to fail this class. They think I'm fat. They think I'm ugly. No they don't. They don't care.

I'm hungry. Am I hungry? What should I have for lunch? I shouldn't have much because I'm fat. It's better to have a big lunch and a small dinner. What time is it? Has this class nearly finished? I can't wait to get home. I can't wait to be safe again. I hate being outside. It's so threatening, anything could happen.

Why do I think that? I shouldn't think that. What am I going to do for the rest of the day? I'm exhausted. I want to sleep. You can't sleep now, you won't sleep tonight. I should do work. Do I have any work? Yes but not that much. Actually I have loads. I better do my work.

How long have I been doing my work? What time is it? I'm hungry. I should have dinner. I shouldn't eat past 8. I'll just have something small. Am I still hungry? No I'm not hungry. You can't eat you're too fat. Will I finish my work tonight? I need to finish my work tonight. I'm sleepy. What time is it? What time do I need to wake up tomorrow? Will I get enough sleep? I should sleep now.

Why am I still awake?

What time is it?

1,2,3,4 ...

'Prisoners of Our Thoughts': James' Story

Name: James Paintin
Age: 26
Condition: Borderline Personality Disorder
Location: Rugby, Northampton, United Kingdom

"The thing with borderline personality is ... everything is black and white, there are no grey areas. My story starts with the most powerful love. The love only someone with BPD can give. The most total love.... But with the most powerful love comes the most powerful fears ... the worst nightmares ... terrifying paranoia. At the time, there seemed only one way to fix this imbalance: medication. Though partly zombified on these new meds, I very quickly found that my life was passing me by in a daze. I was there but absent. And what did my partner do? Feeling abandoned and insecure, she went elsewhere. I lost everything. Increasingly, I became a walking dead person. I tried to die. I just couldn't. Nothing worked. I stopped seeing my kids. I was shutting down. I got to the absolute point of being done with life.

Being put away from society was probably what I needed to restart myself. Remember who I was and be OK by myself and not centre my life on someone else. Maybe the lies were meant to protect me? But liars end up lost in their lies. They also make mistakes. By 2016, after more lies and confusion than I could shake a stick at, I found myself finally being institutionalised. The below is an entry from one such day inside ... "

May 16th 2016

As a group of hooded figures gather outside our five bedroom detached house, adrenaline is pumping through my veins and I decide to peek through the crack in the window blind. In the small seven house cul-de-sac the commotion from this group of thugs wouldn't go unnoticed as they cast long shadows under the dim orange light of the street lamp. Somehow everyone in my house, mum, step-dad and sister are oblivious to the brick that has just come through the glass in the front door. I can hear threats of "We are coming for your family". I feel urged to act, I grab a carving knife and run out of the door to confront the large group of

31

strangers. Even as they move towards me it is impossible to make out their faces. They seem pleased I have left the comfort of my house until … I plunge the 10 inch blade into the first guy's abdomen, blood spurting from the wound. The others seem incensed and charge for me. With one swift motion the blade hits another's neck, slicing through it like it was butter as his head falls from his shoulders and thuds onto the floor, his body slumping over a tree stump. Some of the others run, some seem stuck to the spot. I feel in control, as my actions return to me and my breathing calms. Looking at the scene of the massacre I wonder what has just happened as my step-dad emerges from the house, angry at the commotion. I try to explain what has happened but he flies into a rage, concerned what the neighbours will make of all the noise.

He picks up a shard of glass and comes for me; I run, but my legs don't seem to work. I turn to him and out of his reach he throws the shard. I look down just at it sinks into my torso, blood drenching my t-shirt. My mum has arrived and is hysterical, I can't bear the noise. I try to explain to her what's happened, that he's tried to stab me for only attempting to protect them. Though by the time I have finished she is persuaded that I am in the wrong. Feeling the world closing in on me I make a run for it; my step-dad tries to follow me but my mum stops him. I need to escape this man, I think to myself, otherwise he is going to kill me. Terrified, I run over the top of the house, tiles falling from the roof as I go. "That's it," I think. "I'm on my own now."

I wake up, in a cold sweat, petrified of my dream. How real they feel is crazy. I lie there trying to focus on reality. My knuckles are blooded; I punched the wall whilst I was in my nightmare. This time I'm thankful I've woken up. One of the side effects of my meds is drowsiness and I seem to get stuck somewhere between nightmare and reality. It's the most horrific feeling to be stuck, having to seemingly – or so it feels at the time – live through all this bad stuff happening to you, unable to wake up. Your loved ones turn into demons, your demons turn into even worse, you are lost and can't escape.

Going to sleep can be so so scary; this is why I insist on a kiss goodnight, or if I'm not with my partner, a proper goodnight over the phone can help. If I don't get either I will struggle to sleep. If I haven't been able to speak to her, for whatever reason, my head will fill with worry. "Is she in trouble, leaving me, or with someone else?"

The simplest goodnight can stop so much paranoia.

A Day in My Head

My door is unlocked at eight o'clock in the morning, and within seconds there is so much noise outside my door. I need to get up so I can get my medication but getting up is so hard when you feel like you haven't slept. My meds make it so hard to function in the morning. I feel like a zombie, as if I'm not really in my body. It feels like I can see myself, but I'm not in control of myself, almost in autopilot mode.

This feeling can last 10 minutes or three hours, but I've been on too much medication and I've lived months in this zombie state. You can lose yourself, plodding along not really aware of your surroundings.

Getting the right dose is vital to keeping as "normal" a life as possible, but it's just all trial and error. At the moment I seem to have it right: 250mg Quitiapine at night and 200mg Sertraline in the morning. Just enough to ease the voices and stabilise my mood, but not too much that I can't function as a human being! I'll get my medication, have a cup of coffee and get ready to go to the gym. If I didn't go to the gym I would lose my mind, it gives me something to focus on. Sometimes it's a struggle to force myself to go but the endorphins it releases always make me feel better and a lot more positive. I try to go for two and a half hours, four or five times a week.

This morning, there was an incident here ...

You see I'm currently being kept somewhere I don't want to be. Six months ago I was so mentally unwell, all I wanted to do was die. I tried every way I could imagine. I had in my head why this would be best for everyone. People would say "You can do it, you are strong, stay strong" but I've been strong for so long, I've had enough of the hurt and the daily struggle my conditions, Borderline Personality Disorder and Paranoid Personality Disorder, force me to live through. Imagine a flat garage roof, it gets rained on, snowed on and starts to warp, you fix it, it starts to leak and you fix it again. How many times do you keep fixing it, making it strong again. It will never be the same roof it once was. One day it will just give in from the strain, from the damage. People think you can just "be strong" time after time after time.

So I guess I needed to be in here to get my head straight, re-focus and evaluate my life, and I am much more stable than I was. I certainly want to live my life again. But it means I have to share my space with all kinds of people, suicidal, self harmers, murderers, rapists, thieves and druggies. They put us all together, like the result will somehow turn out positive!

I guess it's a sign of a deep though somehow fortunate and unexpected personal strength that I have turned this into a positive thing, many others can't or won't be able to do this. It's no wonder people get lost in the system. So many troubled people, so much violence, bullying, overdoses and self harm, it's all a daily occurrence here, and on top of all that we are limited in the amount of time we can speak to our families and loved ones.

Anyway, so, there was this incident this morning – the lad in question was restrained by eight staff, which meant that the rest of us got locked back up until 11 o'clock. And so I went back into bed and quickly fell asleep until 11 o'clock, at which point we were all unlocked in time for lunch. The food isn't exactly Michelin star, it's full of grease and flavourless, but I have to eat.

Two o'clock eventually comes round and at last I can go the gym. You can fill your time with education, therapeutic activities or a small job for one pound a day. As for support though, on the whole it really is just you, yourself and you! It can be so noisy and loud, the only respite I can get is to hide away in my 10 x 6 foot room.

Going to the gym is the best way I find to quieten the voices in my head, the ones telling me I'm fat, ugly, stupid, worthless, go kill yourself, everyone will be better without you ...

What are these voices like?

When you go to the supermarket next, stop for a moment and listen to the constant noise and chatter, then imagine that's actually in your head and on top of that there's the noise going on around you, kids arguing, music playing or just someone talking to you. Is it any wonder sometimes I seem blunt or appear rude? It's a lot to take in and deal with, at times it's physically painful.

What do you do when you have a voice telling you to kill yourself and why it is the best thing for everyone?

Sometimes I can compromise by, for example, self harming. It can quieten the voices, give me a rest from the constant rabble of abuse I try to deal with every day. Put two kids, one on each shoulder, shouting at each other through your head ... could you cope with day to day life on top of that? Everything can quickly become a constant struggle. My head can be so loud I don't hear someone

A Day in My Head

starting a conversation with me, or I think someone has said something they haven't! People think I'm ignoring them or just not listening. Sometimes I literally have to see someone's lips move to hear what they are saying and try and focus just on that above all the rest.

I get to call my family before we get locked up for the night, and once a week I can have a visit, which is nice but it can also amplify how much I miss them and want to be home.

So as the evening approaches, everything is still, and for the first time since eight o'clock this morning I am alone, in the quiet with just my mind. I will lie here and watch some TV for a while then try to get some sleep. But, once I close my eyes, I know, the real battle begins, and, who knows what I can expect tonight...!

James Paintin has worked for six years within a secure mental health environment and does an abundance of training and freelance support work. You can follow James on Facebook (James Paintin), Twitter or instagram (@heresjmp)

'Prisoners of Our Thoughts'

Stone walls do not a prison make, nor iron bars a cage. Unlike institutional confinement, a life of nurses rooms, patient 'lounges' and officers' wards, the cerebral incarceration apropos to one's own mental condition has no definitive end. Nor is it defined by physical palisades, although it may, in due course, come to be described in exactly those terms. Difficulty leaving one's home, even leaving the bed, under the most burdensome of mental afflictions, is the sad reality for so many of our contributors ...

Name: JB
Age: 64
Condition: Anorexia
Location: Harrogate, United Kingdom
Profession: Tutor and Writer

Most days are the same. I wake early and wait for the rest of the world to wake. Local radio is my comfort blanket. Breakfast is functional. Food is a necessity. I marvel at those who cook, care about food. I live in a rabbit hutch of a flat. I lost my twin here so it is not a happy place. The wrong kind of memories lurk. I'm trying to move but don't have the energy. I feel threatened by the kids in the street and avoid being here. Mondays are ok as at least the weekend is over.... I watch the secure life of my pals and I know I am going nowhere. Anorexia wrecked most of our lives. It took my twin, or rather the side effects did. I try my best to keep going but it's easy to lose hope. I seem to mind things more than ordinary people. Noises drive me mad here. I get through my lessons. The evening stretches endlessly. I don't like evenings. There is a disturbance in the street and I am frightened and fearful. I ring the police and email the housing association but they won't do anything. The day ends around 10.30pm. I don't look forward to the night, as I can't sleep.

Name: Rachel Elizabeth Bailey
Age: 25
Condition: Obsessive Compulsive Disorder
Location: Leeds, United Kingdom
Profession: Support Group Facilitator at Seek Solace OCD Support York

A Day in My Head

It is 9.30pm, May 16th 2016. I spontaneously open my laptop, totally unprepared for literary brilliance ...

To my own amazement, it seems that at the eleventh hour, my desire to join this mental health movement – A Day in My Head – has once again outweighed and outmuscled my OCD restraints. I had only just emailed Aron Bennett and told him I could not write for him on this occasion. I avoid writing because of a past event which created a schema. The short version is, I am frightened of writing things down, in case they might magically come true. The long version is more fascinating and enlightening ... but I wouldn't want to commit that to paper, would I?

And herein lies the problem of OCD. I cringe inwardly upon hearing that phrase we all loathe ... "I'm so OCD!"... BUT the frustration really comes when we can't easily say what OCD *is*. The OCD Bully boxes clever here, capitalizing on our "broken filters", making us obsess about repugnant, upsetting things, that other people rarely *think* about, let alone feel obliged to *talk* about.

7.30am
I wake and the first thing that hits me isn't the sound of a lawnmower outside or the smell of breakfast cooking, it's an intrusive thought. The thought is about the terrible thing I have always feared since being a little girl; a horrible product of toxic worry. And the OCD Bully presses that gun to my temple from the get go. OCD develops in nice people. It seems that whenever I consider myself to have thought something "mean", or acted churlishly, I will be "punished".

A convoluted pathological chain of events ...

I have the day off today. My boyfriend, Tom, is working. He needs the bathroom more than I do ...

"Oh well, me first!" That's a bad thought. Remember what might happen to you as a result of thinking selfishly ...

My mind starts making connections, which develop into compulsions. It goes to my fear of things being written down. I worry that the lettering on anything will magically morph into bad words, to do with my root fear, and come true. What has writing on it in the bathroom? The shower gel!

Awake for five minutes and I've already mentally contaminated something. It will be added to my stash of things that need "dealing with" via a compulsion.

Sigh. When you mentally taint most of the things you come into contact with, OCD is setting you an endless task. I despair at the thought of actually attending to these silly things, as it is a torturous chore. I will now have to schedule a bit of pyromania into my day.

Another ritual is Pure O – negotiating for restitution – to undo the bad thoughts. Due to the dread of fulfilling the compulsion, I try to bargain my way out of it. "If I don't destroy the shower gel, my boyfriend may fall in love with someone else", I say internally, accidentally, intrusively. "Oh no! Take it back!" OCD now has me haggling my way out of a negotiation. Compulsions ricochet off each other within an Obsession's warzone.

I am running 10k in August for OCD Action. I run to clear my head. I have a panic attack on the homestretch. Something goes off in my head.... "You have to run the rest of the way home, or when you destroy what you are hoarding away, it won't be effective". I do what OCD tells me and continue, elevating my heart rate following a panic attack. A doctor would recommend that I don't, but OCD recommends that I do.

I am not psychotic, but when under immense stress, an imaginative person can see things which aren't there. On the way back I experience a distressing psychotic-like symptom. More trickery which gives the OCD more credence, making it even more insidious.

I collapse breathless on the couch. I ring my long-suffering mum for reassurance. I choke as she says, "Rachel, are you crying...?"

It is 9.30pm, May 16th, 2016. Our affectionately named stray Mad Max meows for in. A very vocal Kitty, he makes his hunger known. I have nothing for him. Today when I visited the store, OCD wouldn't let me buy cat food. The label contained a "bad word".

OCD is often looked on as positive ... for increased productivity and efficiency.

Factually, it's utterly disabling and maddening. Today was miserable and unproductive. I go to bed mentally exhausted, finally silencing the constant chattering of OCD.

A Day in My Head

Name: Wayne Power
Age: 32
Condition: Agoraphobia
Location: Waterford, Republic of Ireland

I usually leave the house at 10am. "Leave the house". Still such a novel concept after three years incarcerated at the behest of crippling panic and agoraphobia. I look in the mirror and do my 7/11 breathing: inhale to seven and exhale to 11. My phone and iPod are my weapons as I go into battle the minute the front door opens.

A heatwave, they said. Not that it'd make much difference to me. I have not seen a beach or beer garden in over ten years. It's cloudy overhead. Perfect Monday weather. The bus pulls up across the road ferrying lives. To be on there, sat with a purpose and destination. Someday. Not today. I cross the road and go my usual route. Familiarity breeds contempt despite the safety it offers. Today it prompts boredom and repetition. Same people, same faces, same old, same old. I'm calm for now. I walk up past the local Health Park, and gaze ahead, past the nearest primary school. Today's target to get past the two sets of railings that are separated by its small car park entrance. And then walk back. Unscathed but not unsettled. The anxiety bubbles away in my stomach. It's like an old friend. I get towards the lollipop crossing outside the school entrance. I'm OK. Focused. Just get to the end. That's four houses on the left and three on the right. If I'm adventurous maybe I'll cross the road and walk a few more yards.

I'm at the car park entrance now. The point where an inner conflict takes place. Walk back now before you have a panic attack. No, keep going. Breathe. Don't walk so fast. I walk on past the car park entrance and the anxiety is searing. I fidget with the inside of my coat pocket. My iPod earphones have become tangled in my state of agitation, and just as I near the end of those railings, I bottle it again. The doubt wins again. And then as I turn back towards home the tsunami rises. The black hawk of panic has dug its claws into my back again. My head is a frenzy, replaying the same horror movie I've starred in numerous times. People walk by in a blur. My legs feel detached from my body the faster I walk. The adrenalin and panic is intense. I'm gonna fall down. I'm gonna be on the pavement fighting for breath aren't I? I'll be in an ambulance with a respirator. Faster I walk, letting it do its worst. Pulling out my iPod and scrolling through artists. Anything to distract me, to neutralise this daily threat. My body feels rigid and taut. I feel like I'm in slow motion. And as I get past the entrance to the Health Park, I take another breath.

It's gone. I'm OK. It was three, maybe five minutes. But every second felt like an eternity. I'm OK. It's gone. It'll be back. I'm exhausted and it's only 15 minutes since I left the house. And that sweet relief as always gives way to frustration, deflation and a hollow sadness. Where to next in my little bubble-wrapped, agoraphobic world? Walls and roads and destinations all shielded by panic. Every walk feels aimless.

The sun has come out, glaring down on my skin. I wish for the rays to burn the panic and anxiety to a crisp. People come and go, in shorts and shades and dog leashes. How easy for them to go about their day as they please. I envy them. No restrictions. No fear. And yet if I let myself drown in thinking, it'll overwhelm me. The years lost, the life that should be led. The places I should be going. Not this daily trudge, measuring distances from the front door of my house. I would swap it all for the mundane. To be those waiting for the bus to ferry them to a nine-to-five. To be that passing jogger that runs wherever he likes. Or the sleeping toddler in its buggy, asleep to a world of possibility and promise.

I'll do it. I'll get my life back. I'll banish these demons and watch them turn to dust. Someday. Not today.

Name: Henrietta Ross
Age: 34
Condition: Bipolar Disorder
Location: Scotland, United Kingdom

Hello, Diary. I don't come here often. We no longer have our date at six o'clock, after I close the heavy curtains and breathe a sigh of relief that another day is over.

I used to, do you remember? I used to scrawl countless words every day on your crisp white pages with an old blue biro, but not now. I don't need to read my own thoughts to understand myself anymore. It has been too long.

'Why did you do it?' he asks. I look at him. No other species is asked why they tried to kill themselves, having to explain in grim detail what happened and why, all the while wishing you were now enveloped in that cool objective darkness that you'd set out to discover only yesterday. The idea of silence, complete silence, where this chaotic, deafening world becomes beautifully quiet and

A Day in My Head

the inside of your head becomes beautifully quiet and you lie down, perhaps on the soil in your garden and snuggle up to the silent, musty earth, and close your eyes as you are engulfed by wave upon wave of something resembling peace.

It only seems like yesterday that I sat in that room, biting my fingernails, staring at the wall opposite, trying to avoid eye contact with the giant man who sat in the chair. It has actually been years. I still often want to die; other people meditate or do some light stretches or drink black coffee as their morning ritual, I regularly think about dying and decide which would be the quickest, cleanest way to kill myself.

You can't get away from yourself, that's the problem.

I'm trying to add the finishing words to this article. Wilde once said "I spent all morning taking out a comma and all morning putting it back." It doesn't seem a long unit of time to me – I will probably still be here next month.

I can't have a five-minute break at 11 o'clock from my mind, open a shiny, little red door at the front of my head, like an old fashioned cuckoo clock and swing my tired, forlorn legs out into another dimension where grey matter isn't necessary and we can communicate via colourful, wooden door knobs.

My mind – I feel that it is not so much a fight, or a symbiotic relationship between mind and body, but more my mind dragging me like a paper bag battered by the wind. Twisting and turning, flung high into the air beneath a granite sky that threatens rain. It skims past people's heads, sometimes catching the edge of their surprised faces or a strand of their silky hair as they walk, without a care in the world, down the busy street. It gets thrown at shop windows, finds itself stuck under car wheels for a second, then suddenly falls back down, lies silent, before another gust comes and takes it.

The tiredness, that's the worse, I feel fatigued today, want to retire to bed with a cup of tea and that packet of biscuits my partner bought yesterday, but I can't because I have a list of things to do, a list that never gets any smaller. If I were manic, this would be a breeze, but I'm not manic, I'm depressed. Therefore, everything is too much. I sometimes wonder how we continue to breathe when depressed; depression shuts everything down, and I am often surprised my brainstem has not shut down too.

Maybe I should write this article again.

I wish it would all shut down, including the social anxiety and the other form of anxiety that doesn't have a name as it is a cluster of anxiety types. It doesn't need a name, it just needs to bog off.

Other human beings are the difficult part. Considering it's modern society that makes us sick, it feels unfair that once it has caused the damage, they immediately want to ostracise you. It's almost as if they think you're weak because you faltered and fell while they continued; but who is the sicker in that equation? Part of them has to die to live in modern society. Part of us is too alive.

My partner made me a rhubarb crumble. The crumble is nice, tart, and sweet. It makes me think of the garden, my metaphorical little door into a quieter and more sustaining place. I think I will stop writing. Go and watch the birds, it will help me get out of my mind.

Generation Y(-BOCS)

The demographic cohort succeeding *Gen X* is, in so many ways, more glimmeringly self-aware, more fearlessly informed, than perhaps any generation before them. From school and college right through to university, our younger contributors have proven that they are capable, by turns, of the most darkly wry yet luminously petrifying content. Spellbinding and clear-eyed, these are the lives of our youngest writers who, as well as dealing with every other adolescent concern, must somehow weather the internal windstorm of mental illness; the menacing torment and chaos addling otherwise exuberant minds.

Name: Tifé Adegun
Age: 18
Condition: Depression
Location: London, United Kingdom

"I am too young to be this sad," I tell myself as I walk into my school's library. There are five alcoves situated at the far right of the room, each with a chair and a computer. I choose the last and sink into the chair. I lean my head against the cool wooden table, and my bag drops off my shoulder and onto the floor with a thud that reverberates around the room. An atomic bomb of sadness.

The tears that have been building throughout my solemn pilgrimage to the library surge out of me, wave after wave, and with each silent sob my vision blurs, trapping me in my own little blue world. For someone with anxiety, the risks of being seen to be falling apart at school petrified me, but any reasonable, rational thoughts were struggling to be heard amidst the deafening static in my mind.

Minutes pass, and whilst to passers-by I look like a weary student taking a nap after a long day at school, the storm inside my head grows tumultuous.... The thoughts begin.

"They don't like you."
"They never did."
"You sold your soul to try and fit in and it didn't work."
"You don't belong anywhere."

As a new girl, I had tried, believe me I had *tried*, to keep the old friends that moved schools with me as well as make new friends here. It didn't work. To my friends I was a traitor, to the 'old girls' I was a nobody - how could I compete with people who had known each other for years? I realised soon enough that the 'old girls' pitied me; I tried to brush off the looks when I asked if I could sit with them at lunch. I tried to pretend it didn't bother me when everybody had partnered up in lessons and I was the odd one out. I tried to pretend that I was okay being overlooked, or worse, an afterthought, because it put my anxiety at bay, and if I could pretend I wouldn't have to be realistic.

Well, if reality is an anxiety sufferer's kryptonite, it feels like each tear that falls sears groves into my face, as each tiny bauble of water that escaped carried the burning weight of the same sentence. A sentence that I thought was my crippling reality – "You are not wanted."

"You are not wanted." "You are not wanted." "You are not wanted." "You are not want-"

And suddenly it stops. The voices disappear and the static reduces itself to a steady hum. My eyes feel raw, the weight of my sadness resisting all efforts to open them, to avoid confronting my haggard reflection in the black computer screen. All I can feel now is that familiar, dull ache that pulsates around my body, emanating from my heart. But I know how to make that stop.

I pick up my phone and remove its case. A silver blade clatters onto the table, though I hardly hear it over the pounding in my head. The metal catches the light, making it wink as it falls, as if it knows my secret. I push my skirt up, exposing my upper thigh, thumbing the ridges of old scars that have long since pickled the skin, and skimming the angry red lines of scars yet to form. I picked up my blade, and with the surety of Picasso with a brush I, too, glide my feelings onto my canvas, over and over and over again. As the skin splits with every stroke I feel my mind begin to settle, the static wanes to nothing, and I am at peace. Pain demands to be felt, so I choose pain over sadness.

Name: Theresa Ann
Age: 19
Condition: Unknown (8 unsuccessful diagnoses)
Location: Birmingham, United Kingdom

May 16th 2016.

Monday morning. Is it Monday already?
I haven't slept a full night in the last month.
I can't sleep – I'm scared of what will happen.
I've got a few weeks left before I leave my college and go to university so sleep is vital really.

A Day in My Head

I go to sleep, as usual, sometime between 5.20-5.30am (I can't remember exactly what time I dropped off to sleep) and wake up at the usual time of 6.00am to a growl in my ear.
This is becoming a joke – I just want to be able to sleep and not whimper when I close my eyes.

I've dragged myself to college for an 8.45 start.
Nearly got run over twice. Stupid medication.
I wish they'd just choose a medication and that would be it; the side effects can't be healthy to live with.
Dinner was at 12.00 – couldn't eat. No appetite yet again.
The voices got worse during lessons and the visual hallucinations proceed to ruin my life day in day out.
Have to leave college early.
Get home for 4.30pm instead of 5.30pm.
Get home to be greeted by dinner. Wasn't hungry.

The voices had become the loudest they'd been in ages throughout much of the day, to the point I was shouting at people instead of talking because I couldn't even hear my own thoughts.

The visual hallucinations were trying to get into my window at around 6.00pm.
8.00pm: I really should've had a bath. But I'm scared of something drowning me.
9.30pm: The television had started calling my name so I turned it off, stared at the ceiling for a while then I went to the bathroom.
9.45-9.50pm: The weird looking goblin creature was in the bathroom cabinet again calling my name. When will this end?
10.00pm-2.00am: (Have no idea what went on - went into a trance and cannot remember whatever it was that had transfixed me).

A day in my head is hard. I constantly battle with myself and have delusions that my visual hallucinations will take over my body. Can't seem to shake the paranoia that everyone is out to get me.

Hopefully I should have a full diagnosis by July 2016.
After years of the "professionals" investigating my symptoms and tracking their 'progress'. Then hopefully I'll get a medication that is right for me and actually enjoy life.

Name: Sarah
Age: 23
Condition: Anorexia
Location: Surrey, United Kingdom

Last night was hard. Hunger kept me awake. I read somewhere once that the reason for this is because your body knows it needs nourishment so it keeps you conscious to go in search of it so you don't die in your sleep. Nice, huh? I allowed myself to sleep in a bit in the hope that it would give me more energy to start the day. It didn't. Then I spent a good couple of hours convincing myself that no matter how much my mind tells me I don't need it, the only way I'm going to increase my energy levels is by eating breakfast. I remember when we were little, my parents would buy the variety packs of cereal and my brother and I would fight over the best flavours. Today it was a struggle to consume half a bowl of diet cereal. How things have changed.

It sounds ludicrous, but I can literally feel the weight gain with every mouthful. I try and put on a brave face, especially in front of my family but it's not easy. They wonder why I can't just eat but I can't explain it very well. It's kind of like you're faced with a pan of boiling water and everyone is telling you to put your hand in it but all your instincts are telling you not to. You do it anyway because you don't want to make other people worry. It doesn't stop it burning though. Again and again and again. Yes, you may be dipping your hand in that water like everyone else, but you're also now covered in scars that will need healing too.

I should have exercised today but I was too exhausted. I don't remember the last time I walked up the stairs without having to stop at the top to catch my breath. I don't remember the last time I showered without handfuls of hair falling out. I don't remember when these things stopped being a concern to me. They're just normal now. Another thing that's become almost second nature is lying. My mum came home at lunchtime and asked me what I'd done today. I told her I got up early and had been searching for jobs all morning. I also told her that I'd already eaten lunch. I don't want to lie but sometimes it's easier than facing the truth. I don't want her to worry.

I was desperate to find out what was for dinner as soon as she came in but I didn't ask because I didn't want to sound too eager. I needed to know so I could plan how to get rid of it. Eat in my room and throw away the evidence? Purge? Say I'm not hungry? Eat and

A Day in My Head

feel horrendous guilt? I'm still not sure when the option "enjoy it" was taken away from me. I hope I see it again someday soon.

Name: Roxy Peverell
Age: 22
Condition: Bipolar Disorder
Location: Blumenau, Santa Catarina, Brazil

Part 1

It's 00:22, May, 16th, 2016. I'm in bed with my cat in the darkness, where I've spent the whole day. The sadness is overwhelming. Of course, I'd also spent the day overdosing on sleeping pills, sleeping and self-harming. Nothing seems to work to numb the pain. Death screams in my head. Some friends try to talk to me but they don't understand. It's not that simple.

10:00: What a great way to start the day. Slept and woke up quite early. Nobody's home which makes my mind scream: "Go hurt yourself, go self-harm." Obviously I try to avoid this as much as possible, so I stayed in bed …

It's so incredible how bipolar disorder works.... For three weeks I was on top of the world. I bought a guitar, I dyed my hair blue, I was so determined to be a musician. There was so much hope, I felt strong like I could handle anything and everything. I was exploding with energy … or anger. And now, here I am. At the opposite end of the scale, where all I can think of is suicide. Nothing matters anymore. I just want to sleep forever. And then comes the anxiety, which makes me scared to face the world. Just the thought of going outside makes my heart race.

15:05: Haven't got out of bed yet. Haven't eaten anything. Don't feel the need to. I have to start getting ready for singing class, if I choose to go that is. I don't. Today I think that my voice sucks and that I'll never get anywhere with singing, so why should I try? It's weird and to think that just a week ago I had my life together. I had such high hopes. I had so much energy and now I have none. The worst part is that after the vocal class I have to go to uni and just the idea of facing people from my class makes me cry. We don't get along because they know I'm "different". People in my country don't understand mental illness at all, especially Bipolar Disorder, and it's extremely frustrating. Being Bipolar is a joke, something that everyone is because everyone's mood changes from time to time. THIS IS RIDICULOUS. Depression = laziness. Anxiety =

47

Coward. They think that the diagnosis is this shameful secret that we must hide from others.

Finally, I decide to get out of bed. I'm still feeling dizzy because of the high dosage of sleeping pills that I took. I just wanted to sleep non-stop. I love to sleep because it's like being dead. There's a friend of mine buzzing me on the phone but I don't care to answer. I'm tired of bothering him with my problems. It's basically the same as always: I'm depressed again, wanting to kill myself for no specific reason. Life just doesn't make sense anymore. DON'T GO OUT OF THE HOUSE, my head screams. I try to make my face look acceptable, wear the first thing I see and, almost fainting, I finally leave the house. The sun burns but all I see is grey. Last week everything was so colourful.... It's exhausting; these extreme ups and downs. Oh, to have both together like on the mixed episodes, those are the worst - I just feel more unstable than ever.

So anyway, here I am, all dressed up waiting for the bus but guess what? I lose it completely and just sob … because I'm a failure. And so I decide to stay at home. I know I have important stuff at uni but I just can't go. Normal people don't understand how hard it is. A few weeks ago, staying at home alone would mean listening to songs out loud, dancing across the house, watching TV series non-stop but now I don't have the energy to do those things that I liked the most. Nothing pleases me and that's why I will just lie down with my eyes closed, not exactly sleeping. Just drowning in thoughts. I'll cut myself again just to try to ease my mind. It does work. But self-harming after 10 years is already an addiction and the worst part of any addiction is that you always want more. So I try to stop myself there. The thoughts of suicide gets stronger. I just want them to stop. Since I have no motivation, I'll just stay in bed. Trying to stay alive. Maybe watch some more TV and sleep again. I just wish that people were more understanding of people with mental disorders …

To be continued …

Name: Naomi Lea
Age: 18
Condition: Anxiety, Panic Disorder
Location: Denbighshire/Cardiff, United Kingdom

A day for me is just like a day for any other A-level student. Wake up, go to school, work, get home, revise, relax, and sleep. However, it is not

A Day in My Head

always that simple; there are some added challenges. For you see, I also struggle with anxiety and panic attacks.

Today started for me at just gone midnight. I was still awake because I had too much flying around my head. *What do I need to do tomorrow? My first exam is really close, how will I cope? I need to sleep otherwise I won't get any work done.* It is a vicious cycle of little sleep on the one hand but sheer exhaustion on the other. I got around five hours sleep in the end. An improvement on other nights.

7:00am my alarm went off. Time to get ready for school. Today I woke up, like most days, feeling sick with anxiety about the day ahead. Overthinking again. My brain never stops. I had to slow myself down, stop for a moment. My morning routine includes everything "normal": get dressed, do my hair, brush my teeth, pack my school bag and leave the house. Though I also have to add in a session of relaxation in the morning. This varies everyday depending on what suits me best. Today's was just some mindfulness to bring me back to the present. Only then can I get ready and leave for school. *Breathe in, breathe out. How will I cope today? What happens if I have a panic attack? Is today going to be a good or bad day? What if my friend isn't in this morning?*

Finally I got to school and my anxiety levels subsided a little bit. I started talking about Eurovision with some friends. There were mixed opinions as usual – some loved it and others hated it. *What will we be doing in biology this morning? Have I done all the work I needed to do? What if she goes over a past paper and I don't know the answer? What if I freeze and have a panic attack in front of everybody?*

A morning of biology and a mixture of taught lessons as well as self-study. This brings its own challenges for me, as when I am struggling concentration doesn't come easily. My mind drifts off. *What are things like at home? When will my next CAMHS appointment be? I really need it.*

Then it hit me – a panic attack. I wasn't in a lesson so I just got up and walked away. *I don't want anybody seeing me like this. I feel sick. I'm shaking. My mind is racing. I can't do this.* I got to the toilets and locked myself in a cubicle. It's one of the only silent places where I can have privacy. I start to cry. It's like that feeling when you miss a step on the stairs – but it doesn't go after a few seconds, it carries on. *Breathe in, breathe out. Slowly and deeply. I need to speak to someone.* I decided to go talk to my learning mentor - she has been a great support the past few months and she will help me calm down. I don't always remember how to calm myself during a panic attack, so teachers know what works for me and can suggest things when my mind is blank. We sat and talked about what made me panic and what she could do to help. Finally I was calm again and ready to go back to studying.

The day carried on like that. Mostly calm. Every so often I would become increasingly anxious but I could calm myself down. *I will be fine. It is going to be okay.* Finally home time came. A relief for me. This evening was time for some well-earned self-care in the form of working on and adding to my recovery book, a book I created to help me when I'm struggling, full of positive memories and quotes to motivate me.

Then bedtime. Yet another restless night ready to do it all over again tomorrow. A day in my head is exhausting at times. I could easily wish to swap heads with someone else, but most of us have our own battles even if we don't show it. We all have different hurdles to overcome and mine are created by my anxiety and panic attacks. But I'm okay with that.

Name: Emily
Age: 18
Condition: Obsessive Compulsive Disorder
Location: Dartford, United Kingdom

Today was a good day for me. I was still anxious about all of the contamination I could come into contact with, but I was calmer than usual and didn't feel like I was going to have a breakdown. I'm currently studying for my exams which begin in June so my stress levels are higher than normal, meaning that, despite it being a good day, it was also pretty typical as far as symptoms go; I washed my hands about 15 times before I left the house, put my hand sanitizer on six times during school (slightly less than usual) and then lost count of how many times I washed them after school. My thought patterns were also pretty typical, thinking about what contamination I was coming into contact with, having irrational fears and imagining different catastrophic scenarios.

As an 18-year-old, I find it quite hard to express how Obsessive Compulsive Disorder affects me as there is so much stigma around it, especially with young people. How can I explain to people that I think I am going to die if I don't wash my hands or that perhaps this or that object has got the swine flu germ on it? How can I tell people that I'm currently imagining how I would escape if a gunman were to come into my school? People can't comprehend that I go to sleep every night thinking that I might wake up with my mum dead. My head is constantly filled with thoughts of danger and fear, they are so consuming that I am physically exhausted, feeling worn out by about 3pm each day and falling asleep watching TV in the evenings.

A Day in My Head

Today was no different from the rest. I feel like I have become so accustomed to my obsessions and compulsions that I am a robot; the doctor described me as having severe OCD that is 'high functioning'. Although, I think since starting my Sertraline I have become better at functioning.

My obsessions are based mainly around contamination fears and catastrophic events taking place. My compulsions take the form of large volumes of hand washing, disinfecting and tapping my head. So today when I imagined my mum having a car crash on the way to work (I don't intentionally think of these things, they just pop into my head), I tapped my head on the left side as I usually do. When I touched the bin this morning, and every other time I touched it today, I washed my hands. The bin is my ultimate obsession. No matter how many times I watch my mum disinfect it or even disinfect it myself, I still have to wash my hands; I even make my family members wash their hands too to stop me having an overloading feeling of panic. When I got home from school I completed my usual ritual of going straight upstairs, using my elbow to open my wardrobe and putting my bag down, going into the bathroom and washing my hands, getting an antibacterial wipe and wiping my ring, glasses, any other jewellery and then finally my hair. Following this, I immediately changed into my pyjamas to make sure that I was free from contamination and could therefore continue with my evening with as minimal stress as possible.

Despite being described as high functioning, I still feel like every single day is a constant battle. New thoughts are circling my head causing me to obsess and then develop new compulsions; at the minute I'm currently panicking over the fact that it is now warmer weather and my mum will put my clothes on the washing line. I've already made it clear that I can't have my pyjamas on there this year because germs will get on them. Luckily, I have such a fabulous support network and my mum is my rock. It's so hard for me to cope with each day and maintain my studies but somehow I find a way to make it through. My head is on constant overdrive but I'm sure I'll eventually get through it.

Name: Sam Barakat
Age: 18
Condition: Depression
Location: London, United Kingdom

I wake up to go back to sleep. This continues until I finally wake up properly. Mind empty. As I stare out of my window it dawns on me that I was meant to leave 20 minutes ago. Do I get up? No. I just continue to stare into blankness. When I walk into school, people act like they know me: "You're always late", "Ever heard of an alarm clock?"; "Wow, only 45 minutes late, that's a record". They don't know what it takes for me to get myself out of bed each morning. They don't know what's going on in my head. I shrug their comments off and continue my day. I struggle to concentrate in class but I manage. Lunch time comes by rather quickly. I sit at the lunch table alone. Near to me are a group of 10 people from my class. They are close enough that I manage to hear their conversation. "What do you mean the shop ran out of popcorn? I might as well kill myself!" Little do they realise that I've wanted to kill myself.... They also don't seem to realise suicide isn't a joke. What is a joke though is society's portrayal of mental health.... Before I manage to overthink this, Rosalyn walks up to me. She starts talking to me:

Rosalyn: Hey, you done the English?
Me: Yea haha, thanks to Wikipedia
Rosalyn: Haha oh my god, same.

We both laugh. We weren't meant to use the internet but we both did. We then chat about this new TV series, *Girl Pearl*. We end up laughing so much that Mr Franks tells us to quieten down. Afternoon classes go very slowly, with all of us waiting for the school bell at the end of the day. As soon as the bell goes we all run our own ways. I head to the library to complete my homework then I go to the shops for a few hours. I arrive home at around 9pm, where I have dinner, get ready for bed, then sit in bed with my mobile phone and laptop. And then ... it starts.

I just stare into space. I have so many things to do. English essay. Maths revision. House chores. But what do I do? Nothing. All I do is procrastinate. Thoughts enter my mind. Negative thoughts. Thoughts of suicide. Memories of all the defective things I have done. Blaming myself for things that were not my fault. Overthinking past experiences, thinking about how things could've changed, both in a good way and a bad way. I make up scenarios in my mind. Some happy – meeting somebody whom I marry and spend the rest of my life with, winning the lottery, talking to somebody whom I've not seen for five years. Some not so happy – arguing with my teacher and ending up expelled, somebody in school finding my diary and reading all the negative things I write and then showing everybody. I try to distract myself by thinking about how the day has gone. I managed to do some work in class. I handed in my homework. I had a laugh with Rosalyn ... but my

A Day in My Head

mood soon shifts again. When my class joked about suicide. Why do people joke about suicide? Do they know what it's like to be suicidal? Last month when I felt like I'd be better off dead. They don't know how it feels. I've been there and I know how hard it is. When I used to think of ways to hurt myself with anything I see around my room. When I cried myself to sleep.

I try to put my thoughts to one side. I go on my phone. I see semi-nudes of perfect bodies on Facebook. If only my body looked like that. I then see a photo from my birthday party two years ago … back when I knew what happy meant. I start to think of all the happy things that happened that year. I smile for a second then continue scrolling. I see another photo and I just stop and stare at it. I read it multiple times, taking in what it is saying: "Smiling depression. When you are so depressed and empty, but you hide your feelings with a smile. Nobody knows just how depressed you are". One smile can hide everything. I know this because I've been depressed for two years and nobody even knows …

All In a Day's Work

Whilst some may be confined by their illness (and this is no slight on them), others remain high functioning. They work not only for themselves (and in spite of often great adversity) but on behalf of us all. Their stories are often most remarkable:

Name: Hollie
Age: 28
Condition: Borderline Personality Disorder
Location: Birmingham, United Kingdom
Profession: Service User Consultant

My day began with desperately trying to drag myself out of the Quetiapine fog that so often inaugurates my mornings. I struggle to sleep without medication; as much as I would prefer not to take it, being awake for 2-3 days at a time isn't all that conducive. It takes a good 20 minutes for its sticky, treacle-like grasp on mind and body to slacken and I feel almost human again. Almost.

I need to hand in an assignment at university. The fears of it not being good enough, of being a failure and a fraud rush to the surface. Being told you'll never amount to anything or have any worth stays with you; at 28 and in my second year of university those things still haunt me. At university I see a gaggle of students waiting at the submission desk, all in their early twenties, all handing in their dissertations. I resist the urge to slap them all. Being a mature student makes you bitter. I wonder what life might've held in store for me had I not been 'ill' at their age.

Anxiety bites as I make a phone call for work. Delivering Personality Disorder training nationally is an amazing job, which I love. It's the preparation that's often the hardest part. I'd much rather email than talk to someone I don't know over the phone; that way I have solid information I can refer back to if needs be and I don't have to act like I'm super confident whilst what they can't see is that I'm sweating and feeling massively paranoid about how I'm coming across; knowing I'm utterly unable to retain information about directions or rooms they have given me. That also makes me feel like a failure and that I'm bad at my job, and so the self-criticism begins.

I drive from Birmingham to Preston where I'm working tomorrow, thinking about work and writing this. It makes me think of how much my life has changed over the past three years since leaving

A Day in My Head

my group therapy programme. How it was only five years ago that I struggled to leave the house alone, lived from crisis to crisis, and every time I awoke, wished I hadn't. And, how irrespective of all the shit that life has thrown at me – and despite the day-to-day battles with myself – I'm still here.

Recovery is contentious. For me, I don't feel the term recovery really encapsulates my experience or growth. Having Borderline Personality Disorder, it's pretty difficult to think about recovery in the conventional sense. I don't recall a period of wellness before illness. My 'illness' is a product of my life experiences; it's all I have ever known. What have I got to recover? 'Discovery' would be a better though wanky way to describe my experience. I've discovered who I am beyond those life experiences and how to adapt to my surrounding world. Recovery also suggests a finality I do not think is useful. I take steps backwards all the time, but it's the learning in between steps that's the most valuable, not the rigid and fixed idea that once you've experienced a period of wellness you're 'cured'.

I function and I manage. There are still times where I am left utterly blindsided by the intense emotions I feel and I still fuck up more times than I'd like to admit to. Some days I feel almost infant-like – the world is that much of a mystery to me, but I'm learning. Delivering training to clinicians helps me understand my life experiences and myself more each time I go to work. I feel incredibly fortunate for being able to do that. It's not just self-indulgence that makes me do the job I do, it's wanting to improve the way people with Personality Disorder are treated. We're often unjustly demonised by the services we come into contact with due to our complexities. Every time I go to work I hope that someone's opinion might be changed and that someone will receive a more appropriate standard of care because of that. No one deserves some of the experiences I have had because of the stigma surrounding my diagnosis. I don't want to just tell parts of 'my story' – I want to make a difference.

Tomorrow will be the same battle of trying to bring myself into consciousness and away from self-doubt, over-analysis and loathing, but I accept that that's okay.

Name: Norman Lamb
Age: 58

Location: North Norfolk, United Kingdom
Condition: Mental Ill Health, Learning Disability, Autism
**Profession: Liberal Democrat MP for North Norfolk, and
former Minister of State for Care and Support at the
Department of Health**

My day starts with a meeting in Norwich supporting constituents
who have an adult son with autism. They are at their wits end. He's
not getting the right care and support. Budgets are under pressure.
Mum and dad feel that no-one listens to them. I hear this time and
again from the families of those with severe and enduring mental ill
health, or a learning disability or autism. People too often treated
like second-class citizens, not given the same right to treatment on a
timely basis as those with a physical illness or disability.

Most days I devote a big chunk of my time to campaigning for
equality for those who suffer mental ill health and today is no
different. Tomorrow morning I leave Norfolk early to visit a
fantastic social enterprise in Bedfordshire which provides support
for teenagers with a range of mental health problems. I want to
learn and understand more about their work.

I'll then travel to Westminster to meet Bryony Gordon, a journalist
for the Daily Telegraph. She wants to interview me about what has
motivated me to campaign for people with mental illness. I will tell
her about our family's experience. Our oldest son was diagnosed
with OCD at the age of 16. Like so many other families, we were
let down by the NHS, having to wait far too long for treatment. But
the scandal is that, while we could afford to get help for our son
outside the NHS, most people can't. I can't justify that and it makes
me determined to change things.

Mental health affects the whole family. We have been through
emotional turmoil. No-one was there to guide us in how we could
support and help our son. We felt we were on our own hoping that
what we were doing was helping him rather than setting him back.
OCD is a pernicious illness. It destroys people's lives. It's very hard
to hear your son say to you, 'Dad, why am I the only person who's
going mad?' Just imagine what many teenagers go through. Still,
despite massive advances, there is stigma about mental ill health.
Too many teenagers feel unable to seek help, suffering in silence.

So the more we get mental health out into the open, the better. As it
emerges from the darkness, and more people feel able to talk about
it, the pressure on government grows to end the neglect of our
mental well-being. It's extraordinary that 75% of children who

suffer mental illness get no help or treatment at all. Too often services set outrageous thresholds for admission to treatment, turning people away because they are not ill enough. Yet we know that the sooner you intervene, the more likely you are to achieve results.

Later, I will visit Tavistock and Portman Foundation Trust, which is doing incredibly positive work with young people. The reason for my visit is that I am chairing a commission on children and young people's mental health for the Centre Forum Think-tank. I had set up a Taskforce when I was a minister. The aim was to establish a blueprint for the long overdue modernisation of children and young people's mental health services. The report, *Future in Mind*, was published shortly before the election. Somehow we have to maintain the momentum for reform. More investment and a greater focus on prevention are central to addressing the dreadful failure of care which persists. The moral and economic case for ending this neglect is overwhelming.

This diary entry would not be complete without mentioning the West Midlands Mental Health Commission I am currently chairing. Our focus is to look at the cost of mental illness to the West Midlands economy, and explore how we can make better use of public funds to achieve improved outcomes and boost the economy. We are looking at the role of employers, housing, and the criminal justice system. How can we help people with mental illness to find or stay in work? How can we divert people away from prison and into treatment?

It's a big opportunity to make an impact on people's lives. It's enormously time consuming. Every day I'm making phone calls, sending emails, meeting people, trying to shape our recommendations.

It is, in many ways, very frustrating now that I am out of government. But I am doing everything I can to maintain the pressure for change. My days are long and exhausting but I am on a mission and won't give up.

Name: Camilla d'Angelo
Age: 26
Location: Cambridge, United Kingdom
Profession: Research Student

It's 9am and I've just arrived at work. I grab a quick coffee – there's always time for that – and then I head down to the lab.

I am a behavioural neuroscientist at the Department of Experimental Psychology at Cambridge. My work aims to understand the neural basis of compulsive checking. Despite being one of the most common symptoms of obsessive compulsive disorder (OCD), we still don't have a good understanding of the brain mechanisms that lead to excessive checking. I want to know how and why checking develops, and whether there are important triggers. A better understanding of the changes in the brain that cause compulsive behaviour in OCD will lead to better therapeutic options. This is important because OCD can lead to severe suffering, and current drug treatments are only effective in approximately 40-60% of patients.

So what does a typical day in the lab for me look like? Today I spent about 4 hours at the bench collecting data. I work with rodents, so in my case this meant running around the lab, putting rats in and out of boxes, or *operant chambers*. It's what we use to monitor behaviour. On other days, I might perform surgeries, euthanize animals for tissue, process the tissue, and sometimes set up immunohistochemistry runs. The second half of my day is spent in front of the computer: analysing data (ah yes, the joys of statistics!), reading and writing up my methods (and of course, procrastinating and drinking too much coffee).

My interest in mental health started whilst I was studying for a degree in Pharmacology at UCL. I still remember the day that I first became fascinated with the mind, brain, and how it all works. It was during my third year and I had recently discovered the fascinating world of psychopharmacology – the study of how drugs affect the brain. I remember sitting in a lecture about the effects of drugs like cocaine and amphetamine in mice and what this could tell us about mood and behaviour. I was hooked. I knew there and then that I wanted to study psychology.

For my research, I study the contribution of different brain regions to a new rat test of OCD checking-like behaviour. This involves training rats to "check" – rats press a lever to acquire information about the location of future rewards – and then inactivating parts of their brain to test whether this makes them check more, or less. We can design tests of compulsivity that are tailored to specific symptom subtypes of particular disorders. My hope is that these tasks will improve our understanding of brain disorders in people.

But can we really study OCD in a rat? It is true that rats can't tell us if they are obsessing, or why they are engaging in abnormal repetitive behaviours. However, rat models are important to better understand cause and effect. Brain imaging studies in people with OCD have shown that a circuit between parts of their frontal cortex and a deeper structure known as the striatum is hyperactive. However, human studies are correlational: they do not tell us if activity in this circuit is driving OCD or is a byproduct of it. To test causality it is necessary to alter brain function, but this would be unethical to do in humans. And rodents are proving to be excellent models of components of compulsive behaviours, and they are invaluable for studying the expression of symptoms of compulsion.

It's the end of the day and three coffees later, and I feel pretty exhausted. My P value remained stubbornly higher than 0.05 and the results are inconclusive. Frustration is part and parcel of science and scientific research. But on a good day, I consider myself extremely lucky to be paid to spend my days investigating the inner workings of the brain and participating in the search for cures to a hugely devastating psychiatric disorder affecting our society today.

Name: Jenni Regan
Age: 38
Condition: Bipolar Disorder
Location: London, United Kingdom

I was never a morning person but mornings these days are really not great. Friends and loved ones know now not to speak to me (or even really look in my direction...). This is mainly because I have my 'hit over the head' couple of hours as a result of the strong antipsychotic medication I take every night. As I mainline coffee I often reflect that the cure can be as bad as the illness!

I try to keep an eye on my moods these days as a way of managing my condition so always give myself a score after lunch. Today was a six which is pretty impressive and very rare. Of course the fact that I am feeling so well today immediately makes me anxious that I am on a fast ride to mania, even though I may just be having a good day. It is always in the back of my mind. My condition results in a general depressive state most of the time with occasional breaks for hypnomania or severe depression.

Today I have been working from home. My job is one of the areas that actually benefits from my illness as I work as a media advisor for the charity Mind. This means I read through scripts and story treatments for soaps and dramas and try to ensure that scripts end up as accurate and sensitive as possible (while still existing in the soap world). I don't think I could do my job unless I had personal experience. I try to use experiences from many different people as well as experts but I can often describe how a character may be feeling in a certain situation because I have been there and done that.

I would say that work is one of the positives to have come from my condition. I left over a decade of journalism which was a very exciting, prestigious role but totally shit for my mental health with 14 hour night shifts and being bullied by 'talent'. The media is not a great place for anyone without a very thick skin. Other positives include the incredible people I have met with similar experiences. I have many friends now that I have met through the 'mental health world' and wow, is it good to share!

I wouldn't say that my condition affects my day to day life unless I am really unwell, but it is always a threat sitting on my shoulder. I am lucky to have a pretty decent life most of the time with great periods of stability. I have a job I love, an amazing husband, the best friends a girl could hope for, lovely family and even a gorgeous toddler to keep me busy. Sadly she is probably the one most affected when I become unwell. When I'm ill I will literally go from weeks of rushing around the place, taking her to three or four (or more!) activities per day, always singing, always dancing. To ... lying in bed unable to talk, sobbing and not even able to hold her. I do worry about the effect this will have on her growing up and of course am petrified by the chance I may pass on my illness to her (my sister also has a diagnosis of bipolar disorder). I am very lucky that I have people around me to scoop me – and her – up when times are tough. I also know that I will be as open as possible with her about my illness as she grows up so that hopefully she will never feel any stigma around mental health.

Generally it is an exciting time for mental health – even the royals think we should be talking more about it. I do hope that by the time my daughter is an adult mental illness will literally be considered the same as a physical illness. You never know it might just be some great soap storylines that are the final push!

An Interesting Day

Whilst repetition and routine are often key constituents of a life tormented by mental illness, sometimes – as with any life – the most unexpected events can take place. Hard enough to navigate through such trials and tribulations in full health, let alone with conditions such as Depression and Obsessive Compulsive Disorder to battle with. And it is under these extreme and luckless circumstances that one may be witness to true and unadulterated *bravery*.

Name: Hope Oxley
Age: 24
Condition: Depression
Location: London, United Kingdom

London, UK. 07.00hrs

Oh god, my alarm. Why is it so loud? Why am I so thirsty? And my head, my head hurts so much. Oh no, uh oh. I'm definitely hung over. I am one million percent hungover. I grasp around for my phone, desperately trying to shut off that horrifying alarm sound: BAHH BAAHH BAHH.

Today is the day that my rapist goes to court to announce his plea.

Today is the day that my rapist will inevitably plead 'not guilty', which means that today is the day that I have to prepare myself with the knowledge that I'm going to have to attend trial. Yesterday was the day that my housemate took my hand and got me so drunk that I couldn't see. We laughed and cried and danced and cried some more, because that's what friends do when you're going through something; they help you vent.

I'm working from home today, so I can definitely sleep for one more hour.

London, UK. 12.30hrs

I've washed, eaten and consumed roughly 78ltrs of water and I think I'm almost human again. My office manager has called to check that I'm OK, which I am (kind of). The deputy MD of the company, who, incidentally, has been trying to manage me out of the company for about five months, decided that she wasn't happy about me working from home today and has severely kicked off. Apparently I'm AWOL.

That's the thing with mental health, if you can't see that something is physically wrong, it's difficult to comprehend. But the pressure of a court case, dealing with the fact that your rapist was one of your friends, that you live in a place where you have no family – that's a lot to deal with. That's a lot of strain on your well-being. That's a lot to work with, even without the added pressures of a high stress job. But my deputy MD doesn't understand and thus wants me out.

London, UK. 17.00hrs

I've just got back from the gym. OK OK. So I probably shouldn't have gone to the gym,
but I didn't have a lunch break y'know. My gym is about a mile away and I always walk there, it's pretty suburban where I live and I like the fresh air. I live with five other young professionals in a large house, with a relatively clean roof top terrace. We all have strict routines (it's so strict that we have allocated bathroom slots) which means I know that soon they'll all start filtering through the door.

The daily grind of London life means that a lot of your time is spent wondering why you're packed onto a tube under someone's armpit not being able to breathe. That's why I walk as much as possible, clears your mind. Plus, London is also one of the most amazing, diverse cities in the world, it's nice to actually see it.

London, UK. 19.00hrs

His plea was 'not guilty'. I'm going to court.

London, UK. 20.00hrs

My housemates and I are sitting in the living room talking about veganism (I've been vegan for six weeks and it's a hot topic) and about the differences between vegans and meat eaters. It's cosy in our living room, with old worn leather sofas decked with cushions; there's an abundance of handmade wooden furnishing crafted carefully by our landlord and slightly tarnished lino flooring. My housemates are strewn across the sofas with a level of comfort that

A Day in My Head

only true friends recognise; feet across laps, heads leaning on shoulders and phones being thrown from one person to another to look at the latest laughing meme.

I'm happy. These people make me feel happy. And safe.

London, UK. 23.00hrs

I'm wrapped up in my comfortable, soft duvet, drifting slowly to sleep. I'm crying. I'm crying because today was the day that my rapist pleaded 'not guilty'. My old friend pleaded 'not guilty' in a court of law and I'm going to have to face him again. I'm crying because life is confusing and hard but mainly because sometimes, it's OK to cry just because.

Depression isn't all consuming all of the time, it will always be with me, but it doesn't make me who I am. I have depression, but I understand the difference between being depressed and just being a little sad. If I can recognise my internal struggle, then society should be able to recognise that the internal struggle exists.

Name: Emma Lyn
Age: 25
Condition: Bipolar Disorder
Location: Boston, MA

On May 16, 2016, I woke up around 8:00am, ate a waffle, grabbed a coffee at Starbucks, and went to work at a job I love. It was an average day at work; nothing particularly great, but generally a good day. After work I headed to my best friend's apartment for a girls' wine and cheese night. This was my first time meeting many of her friends because I've been in graduate school and haven't had much time to socialize. However, last week I graduated with my Master's degree so with my new free time, I am trying to take advantage of these social opportunities. Finally, I came home and greeted my boyfriend of five years and cat of three years with a huge embrace. How was my day? It was fine.

On May 16, 2016, my alarm went off around 8:00am. I rolled out of bed around 8:20am and, feeling a bit nauseous, ate a waffle. I looked at the clock and realized I could probably sleep another hour and still make it to work on time. I was exhausted. I felt like shit. I went back to bed. An hour later, my alarm woke me up. I was out the door about ten minutes later, choosing to make time to get a coffee at Starbucks at the sacrifice of taking the time to make myself look presentable.

Work was fine; nothing particularly good or bad, but I was "out of it" all day. I found myself dazing off while talking to coworkers and praying they didn't notice.

My best friend texted me about the girls' wine and cheese night she had invited me to. Shit. I forgot about that. I would have spent more time on my hair, makeup, clothes, everything if I had remembered. On my drive there I began feeling anxious. I decided it was safer to dig around in my purse for a Klonopin while driving than to continue driving with my hands shaking on the wheel and my foot shaking on the pedals.

The girls' wine and cheese night was lovely; my best friend is an amazing hostess. I met her friends and forgot each girl's name before being introduced to the next girl. Everyone was nice and, although not dressed up, was wearing light, just-enough-to-bring-out-your-features makeup, with clothes that looked effortlessly smart. I tugged at my jeans, t-shirt, and beat-up shoes. I was acutely aware of my messy hair and lack of makeup. As was later confirmed during our friendly chit-chat, each girl looked as if she regularly attended barre or spin classes. I couldn't remember the last time I attended a fitness class. One girl was skinnier than me; that bothered me. If I can't be the prettiest in the room, at least I'm usually the skinniest. I wasn't this time.

I tried to smile and be friendly. I tried to participate in the girly, yet still intellectually stimulating, conversation. I simultaneously felt sick from anxiety and just plain sad for no identifiable reason. I knew that I wasn't smiling as much as I should have been, but I couldn't bring myself to care. I was desperate for someone to say that they had to go so that I could follow lead.

Finally, I came home, took a deep breath, and buried my face into my boyfriend's chest. He held me for several minutes, knowing that I needed his warm embrace. Our cat rubbed against our legs. I picked him up and held him tightly for a few seconds. It was a relief to be home. So, how was my day? It was fine.

Name: Abigail Christina
Age: 28
Location: Birmingham, United Kingdom
Condition: Schizoaffective Disorder
Profession: Adult Entertainer/Business Owner of an Escort Agency

A Day in My Head

So my day started just like any other, drowsy from meds and my brain trying to make my body rush as I'm running late and will have a client here in … *40 minutes.*

1pm. So that's him done, nice and easy. Just the usual hour. Need to clean off my latex dress ready for the next.

2.15pm. Okay ... that was a weird 30 minutes. This one didn't say a single word, just gave me my cash and asked to be left for 5 minutes. When I returned back to the room, he was on all fours wearing nothing but a saddle. So what do I do? I get on that saddle and ride like there is no tomorrow. His watch beeped, times up, says thank you and he leaves. And at last I have a bit of time to myself which is consumed by my train track thoughts. You know, those thoughts that feel like a train going past you far too fast? Well *I* know what I mean anyway…

4pm. My work is quiet so time to put on my cat onesie and play with my pride! Believe me, this isn't the craziest thing I do.

A thought attends; as I'm writing this, I'm reflecting on the 28 May 16ths I've had. Most people don't remember specific dates but I actually do. I have schizoaffective disorder and for two May 16ths I was under a section, learning how to be human again. My heart and head leave me in the worst places possible. I always think I'm cured. I always think it's just a phase. Then the voices come back. They creep in slowly but oh so surely. They are there until I start the medicinal concoction again. What do I choose? Drugged up or fucked up? To live long or live free? Well if nothing else, I'm okay for now.

7pm. Well now I'm excited as I'm about to start a booking with my favourite client. Known fondly as '4th Drawer Down' due to the fact that when he gets very excited he screams for the massive rubber fist I keep in my drawer to be brutally rammed into his derrière. And besides, he always likes to party with gin and my favourite white substance.

9.30pm. Well I'm glad that's over, as much as I enjoy spending time with Mr 4th Drawer Down, I'm now feeling a bit worse for wear and needing to wind down for the day. Funny how you never realise how high you are until you feel the low. One minute I'm living my life through upbeat music and the next I'm sitting in silence thinking about how all of my emotions are thought out and scripted, less about how I feel, more about how I depict it.

You see the thing about mood stabilizers and the rest is they are easy to blame for not feeling. Easy to throw in as an excuse for your actions. When really, I'm just a little girl in a grown woman's body. Desperately wanting someone to fill my cracks with understanding, with love, with patience. Maybe it's not a diagnosis I needed but a time machine to go back to when life was simpler. To live a different life. To be better. But in the dead of the night when all is still, I remember that the greatest sound in the world is my own heartbeat. Because even when the whole world has left me for dead, it assures me I'm still alive.

Name: Rachie
Age: 27
Condition: Anxiety
Location: Aldershot, United Kingdom
Profession: Ambulance Driver

Working in the ambulance service and having a mental health condition can be pretty tough. Trying to balance the anxiety I experience as part of my normal day to day living, along with the anxiety caused by being sent to a person with a confirmed cardiac arrest is one of the most difficult challenges I face every day. I always thought that working in this industry, my colleagues would be understanding in regards to my condition and the struggles I can sometimes face. Mostly, they are very supportive and understand when I'm having one of my off days. Unfortunately, not every colleague is always quite so understanding ...

Today I was working with a guy that I have worked with many times before. I wouldn't say we were friends, but I felt like we had a mutual respect for each other and thus were able to work alongside one another with few problems. Apparently, I was very wrong. Today was one of my off days. I woke up feeling twitchy, worried about leaving the house and the usual nauseating knot in my stomach. Nevertheless, I was determined not to let this beat me. I got myself to work and started my shift as normal. (I should point out here that not all of my crew mates know about my anxiety. I am normally pretty good at managing it and I have meds to get me through the really difficult days.) I was restless, legs twitching and hands shaking. We got a job pretty quickly, and I could feel the usual rush of adrenaline that comes with every radio call. Today, that was just too much and so as soon as I got in the truck I took my meds out. My colleague saw what I was doing and asked what was up and why was I taking medicines. I am not worried about who knows that I have anxiety problems and so I quite openly told him why I needed my meds.

I have never seen anyone react in the way my colleague did today. I have had questions like "How do you manage in this job?" before and they don't bother me anymore. I explain that it helps me empathize with my patients and if I let it stop me from doing my dream job then I have let the condition win. I will not let that happen ... I was not prepared for the way in which my crew mate reacted. He started by asking me, "Why the fuck

A Day in My Head

are you at work today?", followed by, "If I knew you were a fucking head case I'd have gone sick today." I was in total shock. Trying to stay rational when I am having an off day can be pretty difficult in its own right, but to then be shouted at by my crew mate was just too much. I shouted. I shouted louder than the sirens we had blaring outside the truck. I shouted at him that I didn't ask to suffer with anxiety, I wish I didn't have to take my meds and that I wish there was an off switch for when I felt like I did. I had to stop myself there otherwise I would have gone on for hours. My crew mate sat there in silence and after what felt like an eternity said, "Well if I'm ever put down to work with you again, I expect you to go sick as I won't work with nutters like you."

I managed to see out the rest of the shift but it was a real struggle. I never expected anyone in the ambulance service to have that sort of attitude towards those dealing with a mental health condition on a daily basis. The statistics state that one in four people have a mental health condition, but in front line emergency services its prevalence is much higher. Be that stress, PTSD or other conditions, it is occurring more and more often. If we can't be supportive of each other on the difficult days, how can we support those that we are purportedly providing the service for on a supposedly routine basis?

Today was a day I'd like to forget, but it is one that will stay with me for a long time.

Name: Jeremy
Age: 47
Condition: Obsessive Compulsive Disorder
Location: Oxford, United Kingdom
Profession: Tour Guide, Performer/Playwright

Get up.

Check my rota. I know I'm due in at 10.30, but check anyway. Just to be sure. Then I think I'm weak for giving into my own doubts.

I have this thing where I can't write or say certain things, because something bad will happen. I want to write a comment on Facebook about the Newcastle United game I watched on Match of the Day last night, but I think, "no I haven't got a right to because I haven't followed the other Newcastle games this season". I know this sounds crazy but...

That Disney song 'Let it Go' keeps popping into my head that's what I need to learn to do. None of these things I worry about are important.

Good weekend, but slightly marred by the fact that I worried that my vision had been damaged. My latest fixation. Whenever I happen to catch a bright light (e.g. the sun's reflection in a mirror) and I find myself dazzled, I panic. On Friday, there I was, stood at the front of the City Sightseeing bus (I'm a tour guide); I gazed absentmindedly through the front windshield for a minute or so, then realised I'd been looking directly at the back-lights of the bus in front. The real worry, in these instances, is that I might face the daunting task of seeking compensation from someone, in this case, my employer. At the root of that is a dread of confrontation and a shame around that dread; I therefore have a habit of inventing difficult situations for myself to 'overcome' – a sort of test. The 'vision impairment' issue was on my mind the whole weekend – whenever I was reading or watching TV – 'do/does the words/TV picture look more blurred than usual?' I wanted to ask my partner for reassurance, but refrained because I thought it was weak and that I will never get better. I even obsess about the *consequences* of asking for reassurance because this is surely an act of weakness which may well be punished.

I've started walking into work. From my house to the city-centre is roughly four miles and takes me just less than two hours. It's a good excuse to listen to music on my ipod (although my sister has warned me it's not safe to walk along with headphones, as it takes away your peripheral awareness). I have this thing about mechanical objects. I lent my ipod to a friend for a Christmas party and when he gave it back I listened to it intently for a good couple of months to see if any damage had been done to the sound quality. Today, walking to work, I notice some 'crackliness' on a particular track. I have to remind myself, 'let it go'. Doesn't matter. So what if it is damaged – so what!

Then on the bus tour guiding, I catch the bottom of my jeans and there is a ripping noise. This could be my worst nightmare. However, I know I ripped them previously on the way to work (they were already frayed). Nevertheless, the thought persists, 'What if I didn't rip them on the way to work - I just imagined that? Do I now have to claim money back for repairs to my jeans from my employer?' Often in life I have to ask myself, 'What would a normal person do?' In this instance, the answer comes back: nothing. *Let it go.* Despite this, I fear that the very thought will not go away. I have to learn some lines from a script this week – what if

A Day in My Head

the jean-tear thought persists to such a degree that I am not able to focus and absorb the words? And yet I know this is flawed thinking; if anything this proves it is simply another obsession and therefore I need to ignore it completely. Many of my compulsions centre around things I am actually afraid or embarrassed to do, so that I feel trapped.

As I write all this, I am aware of how tiny and insignificant these thoughts sound. After all, there are people with real problems in the world. Yet, for me this is real. OCD is my problem. I've often believed we get dealt a hand of cards in life – some good, some bad. Everybody has one bad card and OCD is mine. In other words, everybody has some physical or mental handicap to overcome; this helps me to be more philosophical about it all.

Name: Roxy Peverell
Age: 22
Condition: Bipolar Disorder
Location: Blumenau, Santa Catarina, Brazil

Note to the readers. The journey through mental illness does not begin and end on a single day. Thoughts beget actions, actions consequences. A day after her entry on May 16th, Roxy made an attempt on her own life. The below is something she wrote not long after, which we both felt needed to be shared.

11:37am – May 19th 2016. Finally opened my eyes after hitting the snooze button more than five times. I feel like I was hit by a bus. I think about the day ahead of me and have heart palpitations. Don't want to leave the house. I have to find the strength to take a shower. It's been a week since the last one. For people with depression, even the
smallest things like taking a shower, or brushing our teeth is extremely difficult. We barely have motivation to live, let alone imagining others things. *Luxury* things.

13:42 - I wait to take the stitches out from my suicide attempt. On May 17th I was rushed to the hospital because I was bleeding to death on the toilet floor of a supermarket. The first nurse that I talked with was nice, she treated me well. The problem came later. They couldn't let me leave but, at the same time, the hospitals here in Brazil normally don't have psych wards. And so I spent the entire night on a chair in a waiting room. Anything is more important than a suicidal girl for them!

The next day, I went to see my psychiatrist. It had been two months since the last time I saw him and so I felt we had a lot to discuss. I was wrong. He told me, quite dismissively, that I'd simply done it all for attention, gave me more meds and sent me away. Ladies and gentlemen, that's the public mental health service in Brazil.

14:13 – Stitches out. The nurse wouldn't stop talking about Jesus and how He has a plan for me. I find this annoying because I don't believe in this stuff. But I know he had good intentions and I appreciate the talk. The problem is largely my mother, who doesn't accept that I'm an atheist. Please believe me when I say, I definitely *don't* believe that it's the devil taking control of me. I have an illness (more than one actually), a chemical imbalance in my brain. That's what I believe.

16:45 – Just got out of therapy and now I'm running to get to my singing class. I can feel the crippling anxiety creeping upon me because the bus isn't here yet and I'm going to be late. Can't keep still because of it. Therapy was great, sometimes it's good to talk about our feelings with someone so understanding. We mostly talked about the problems in my relationship. Also she made me draw a tree where people in my life are the leaves, something like that anyway, and it made me realise that I have people who I can count on, that I have hopes and dreams, that I may have a future. Still feel suicidal but slightly more hopeful.

21:13 – I'm at uni now. The singing class was good. I feel that I'm finally improving. This class is more about me building confidence, self-esteem and fighting my anxiety than actually learning how to sing. At the beginning, I couldn't sing alone at all because my fear of failure and negative criticism wouldn't allow me. It still keeps me from doing a lot of things and this comes from the avoidant personality disorder. But today I did it. I sang out loud all by myself. One day I'll be on a stage. One day. Also, had a uni exam today. Had zero motivation to study but I have a good memory and sometimes I can even pay attention to class - so that helped me. I think I did okay, but there's this voice in the back of my head saying that I was terrible. So who knows what to expect. Nevertheless, I am still relatively confident.

Today I felt more numb than sad. But it's a start. Hope. *Onde houver esperança, sempre terá um futuro*. Where there is hope, there is always a future.

A Day in My Head

Name: Zelda Zonk
Age: 45
Condition: Depression
Location: Hertfordshire, United Kingdom

On the 16th May, it dawns on met that it has been two years and two days since my best friend left me. She left silently in the night, hand in hand with cancer, the stealer of souls. The serial killer still at large. She had eaten my homemade pasta the previous day, and we had plans to see each other at 9.30am. Well, I saw her, held her hand, kissed her goodbye but she didn't answer me. Her beautiful skin, translucent almost. No pain. Just her beautiful self, quiet and calm. We met when we were 11 and we had 30 odd years together, some distant, some intimate. We had an unconditional friendship and we loved liked sisters. I miss her every day. I miss her bear hugs and her honesty. I have not been the same since.

On the 16th May, I find myself in a flurry of thoughts. My mum and dad moved 200 miles away on 30th March and the pain is very real. They could not afford to retire here and, having a wish to be in the South West, they made the painful decision to leave. Never have I felt so distant. Never have I been so long without seeing my mum. It's going to take a lot of getting used to.

On the 16th May, I went to the dentist for a filling. I'm disabled due to severe arthritis and I battle daily with pain, immobility and frustration. My dentist is up three flights of stairs. I sat in the car for a while getting my courage together, partly just for getting out and allowing people to see me struggle to walk, and partly for getting up those bloody stairs. At the top I always go to the loo, catch my breath and straighten myself up so I don't go to reception looking how I feel. I'm a master of disguise. A big smile hides big pain. My teeth are not in a good way because of years of sugar addiction. It's my happy place but I need to find a new one. I need to stop comfort eating to hide childhood trauma. I'm in the system for a gastric operation. Terrified. Cross with myself that I can't lose weight and keep it off. But part of me is excited for a big change. I have a great figure in here somewhere.

The 16th May is the day before my son has three big science exams, the biggest yet. My wonderful boy. Turning 15 in June, we have been on our own since he was a baby. My only goal in life when I was younger was to be a parent. To be a mum. I am so proud of him, how he has turned out. He has seen me go through numerous operations, he deals with my daily pain and helps me every day. We have a shared sense of humour that is special and unique. He saved me. And in return I have kept him shielded from how hard it has been, how his dad left us with no money for another woman, and we did not see him for over five years. He does not know that my heart broke. After being diagnosed with postnatal depression, I feared passing the condition on, particularly in light of my own dad having bipolar. I do not speak about any of this to my son. Though as he gets older, I can't hide everything from him. He sees his dad sporadically and we receive some support now, but it is still evident his new family is a priority. Breaks my heart to see his face as he receives another text cancelling plans. Cats in the cradle in the making. My life's mission is to help him be balanced so he can hold his head high and then the chain is broken. So far so good.

On 16th May, after the dentist I went around the beautiful countryside I'm lucky enough to live nearby and took some photos. It's my release, my stress buster. I've only got a bridge camera but I've been approached by a major charity who have shared my work and have a number of followers. I would love to make a living through it but my health needs to be addressed first. I saw some sheep, some bluebells and a cobweb tunnel. Photography breathes fresh air into my psyche.

I go back home, mentally refreshed and ready for my son and the evening ahead.

Name: Av Verz
Age: 38
Condition: Depression
Location: Ipswich, United Kingdom

Having watched the clock throughout another night of insomnia and screaming demons, when it finally hits 06:45 and the house starts to stir, I'm ready to pull the duvet over my head and hide from the world. Though with two children dependent on me, I stick on my "Mummy" face and begin the morning routine of breakfast, school uniform and packed lunch. My eldest is out the door in a loud whirlwind by 08:30, leaving behind me, my husband and my youngest, who is severely disabled and requires 24/7 care.

During the early days of my little lady's life she needed a blood transfusion, and today I am going to finally repay the kindness of a stranger by giving blood for the first time. For years my darkness has stopped me from doing things I've wanted to but today I am determined to fight through my depression and the anxiety that comes along with it. Though there's time for a cuppa first and a catch up of EastEnders. A little bit of Danny Dyer to calm the nerves.

As I drive to the football ground where the blood donor session is being held, my heart is racing and my head is all over the place. The thought of being in a room with lots of people freaks me out; the need to be chatty,

A Day in My Head

smiley and "normal" is a huge pressure, and not being able to walk out when I need to scares me. I don't even give a second thought to the needle or the worries more commonly associated with giving blood for the first time.

We arrive a few minutes early and as we walk to the room I concentrate on calmly breathing and trying to fight every part of me that is telling me to walk in the other direction. The session is busy, people are coming and going and I avoid making eye contact as much as possible. The waiting area is too small for my daughter's wheelchair, so we are allowed to wait outside in the hall; it's quieter and calmer and gives me the opportunity to focus my thoughts on anything other than being where I am.

An hour later and the process is all over, I have officially donated my first 475 mls of blood and managed not to have a panic attack! High five me!

Walking out into the fresh air again, the sun is shining and for the first time in a long while I can feel its warmth. The sky is blue and the world is no longer so intimidating. As I drive back home, I'm feeling something I haven't for many weeks – I think it might be happiness.

The rest of the afternoon passes in a haze of light which, after months of darkness, is a welcome relief. My eldest comes home from school, full of tales about her day and I am able to enjoy her stories instead of not being able to concentrate as is usually the way. My youngest has a fun physio session in which I actively participate, rather than sitting in another room feeling like a useless mother and wondering what the point of my existence is if I can't even find the strength to help her.

Tea time rolls round, and instead of asking the husband to cook something because I don't feel able to, I'm in the kitchen. My eldest daughter comments on the fact that 'Mummy is making dinner tonight'.

After everyone has eaten, I head to the bedroom for some "me" time with my Kindle. It's been a long day and as always I've had to do it on barely any sleep. The more tired I get, the louder the demons are and I'm starting to feel very low again. They never allow me to enjoy the air for long; always ready to pounce on the slightest little dip I have and turn everything black again. I think today though they're just angry because I fought back and, if only for a few hours, I was in control.

Beyond Good and Evil

According to Nietzsche: "The most dangerous of errors hitherto has been a dogmatist error - namely, Plato's invention of Pure Spirit and the Good." Perhaps the most friendly would be to promptly ratify, as Nietzsche goes on to propose, a "transvaluation of all values".

Of course, this is not the view held by the majority of the Agora. For it is surely *religion* and all that faith engenders, which affords perhaps the greatest system of mental succour.

The truth is that mental illness is beyond good and evil. John Moore, bishop of Norwich 1689 was indeed insightful enough, during the age of urban coffee houses and tolerance, to discern religious observance from so-called *scrupulosity*; to distinguish demons from treatable illnesses.

Mental illness is no more about morality than heart disease or pancreatic cancer. Nevertheless, it is hard sometimes not to see our own individual journeys, quite erroneously, through the lens of morality. The striving to be 'good', not to mention the demonic nature of suffering, or in some cases, the abuse or neglect preceding one's condition. It is a struggle many of our contributors must battle with on a daily basis ...

Name: Mitzi VanCleve
Age: 59
Condition: Obsessive Compulsive Disorder
Location: Michigan, United States
Profession: Author of *Strivings Within – The OCD Christian: Overcoming Doubt in the Storm of Anxiety*

"Of all the temptations that ever I met with in my life, to question the being of God, and the truth of his gospel, is the worst, and the worst to be borne." *John Bunyan* [1]

It was during those weeks while I was waiting for my GP to come back that my disorder took the ugliest of all turns. My inability to sit still for very long made it hard for me to relax enough to focus on studying my Bible so I decided that a good alternative might be to listen to some sermons on CD. My son had given me a sermon series that had impressed him and which he wanted to share with me, so I decided to start with those. I figured that I could listen and do other things at the same time to try and distract myself.

A Day in My Head

At first I found the sermons encouraging and insightful but then about mid-way through the series I encountered a sermon that prompted a new obsession that would lay me lower than I'd ever been before. The words of this particular sermon went as follows: "There are a lot of folks who *think* they are Christians but if they are still struggling with sin, then they might not be." *Whoa!* My brain felt as if it might explode in reaction to that statement and a cold fist of terror wrapped around my heart. Those words, when they'd had the chance to sink in, ignited a barrage of horrifying accusations which would soon morph into an all-consuming dread of the possibility of hell and eternal separation from God. *What if I'm not a Christian after all? I struggle with sin in some way nearly every day! What if I've just been fooling myself all along? What if my belief isn't good enough? Maybe that's why I have all this fear and anxiety. Is this God's way of warning me? I need to know. How can I know for certain?* The questions and doubts poured out like water from a burst dam. And the aftermath that this torrent left behind was a deep gouge in my brain of confusion, dread, and incredible sorrow.

This new mental war was far worse than any I'd engaged in before. I wanted to turn back the clock and erase my thoughts. I wanted to unthink these things, but I knew that, short of having my memory erased, that was impossible. These hissing and menacing accusations would come at me relentlessly and I felt that I had no choice but to fight back. I would work very hard to gather evidence against these condemning notions. I would use scripture after scripture to reassure myself that I still belonged to God. Yet every time I'd think I'd won the war, a new question would pop into my head. Often I wished that I could be an animal instead of a human. I would watch a bird sitting in a tree outside the window and think, *oh. . . if I could only be like him, to just instinctively exist without all these questions and doubts and the fear they create. "I said, 'Oh that I had wings like a dove! I would fly away and be at rest'."*[2]

Then, just after that, came the next brutal twist: *atheists don't see themselves as being any different from animals.* The thought leaped up in my mind like the unexpected
charge of a lion out of the midst of the tall grass. *Does this mean that I want to be or actually already might be an atheist?* The question demanded an immediate answer. Indeed, this would come to be the pattern of things. These horrible strivings, no more than a desperate effort to find that one perfect reassurance which I thought could dissolve all my fear and uncertainty concerning my eternal standing with God.

This battle to gain a feeling of certainty about my salvation raged on for quite some time. There were many tangled and twisted turns along the way, but every path led back to one basic fear; eternal separation from God. Every effort or attempt to gain reassurance only led to one more doubt filled "what if?" The harder I struggled against those doubts the greater and more powerful grip they would have on me. How could I ignore these things when to do so might mean the eternal damnation of my soul? How could I find peace when my very own heart condemned me? Later on my eyes would open up to the realization that God's grace and salvation are not dependent upon the fickleness of my emotional states. *"Whenever our hearts condemn us,"* we must remember, *"God is greater than our fears, and he knows everything."*[3]

But first I needed to be educated about *why* I had become so stuck in these obsessive cycles. I needed to come to grips with the fact that I had OCD.

1. "Grace Abounding to the Chief of Sinners," John Bunyan, Penguin Books, Page 83, #1
2. Psalm 55:6 NIV
3. 1 John 3:21 NIV

Name: Walter Wartenweiler
Age: 43
Condition: Mother's Schizophrenia
Location: La Sarraz, Switzerland

Une Journée dans ma Tête: I'm waking up and, like always, I don't think about her but the anxiety of emptiness and abandonment is starting to eat at my bowels and my energy.

Let me start the day by breathing, holding, breathing, holding just so I can get up and light my first cigarette.

She was my mother, she committed suicide when I was nine despite loving me more than anyone ever has since. I'm writing now from 10 years on; 10 years from my most difficult time, and the difference is that these days I am far more psychologically aware. Now, after all these years, I know *why*. She had schizophrenia and her suffering was unbearable; *that's* why she left and not because of me. This understanding is such a relief. And it happened during an insight meditation session where I re-experienced again that night when she jumped out of my room's window. Breathing is what heals me. Breathing my anxiety away, labelling my breath during meditation, feeling it anchor me in the present moment during the whole day ...

This combination of CBT and Buddhist psychology that I learned from great people and apply daily to myself is allowing me to feel finally a bit more free.

I'm finally grieving for you, Mom; it took me 34 years but I'm there. I love you so much.

Name: William Turner
Age: 69
Condition: Depression, Alcoholism
Location: Norfolk, United Kingdom

I'm awake, it's a grand day. Looking forward to my portraiture painting class, meeting like-minded people and forever learning how to paint. Yes – quite a busy day.

In general, I feel relaxed, at peace with my fellow man. My thoughts are pragmatic – 'What do I need to do today?' – and philosophical – 'Without pomposity, can I enhance the lives of others in some small way?'

I am fortunate in my circumstances since I have entertaining, welcoming and supportive friends and family, who all contribute to my preservation of tranquillity. Spiritually I am calm and, as a grandad with five grandchildren, life is exciting and exhausting in equal measure. The future looks good!

This was not always the case, as I am an alcoholic – a recovering alcoholic. I am now able to relax and be mentally and physically calm. Two years ago I was overwhelmed with sadness, anxiety and worry, misguidedly following a course of 'drinking to oblivion' that would solve all! The result was that I was a wreck, broken, finished. I was very good at it, drinking all day and even in the night. The wine bottle could have had 'Poison' written on it – but I still drank it – insanity!

If I drink again it will be one more journey to the asylum and almost certainly a miserable and lonely death. There is intense mental and physical suffering, to oneself and those closest to you, caused by drinking.

I have come to the conclusion that we can alter our lives by altering our attitudes – it's your 'thought life' not your circumstances that determine your happiness.

To reach this reasoned decision required a great deal of help from family and friends. They arranged for me to go to East Coast Recovery (Rehab). This was not a decision I could make for myself – mentally and physically, I was incapable. I lasted a day and a half – I had gone yellow, including the eyes. Looking back, the only difference between me and a Belisha Beacon was that I did not flash on and off! Not good!

The caring staff of E.C.R took me to hospital – there I detoxed and was told that if I hadn't been admitted then in two days I would have been dead. Family, friends and the prompt action of E.C.R staff saved my life. After three weeks in hospital I went home and gathered strength and thought, and then I returned to E.C.R. For me, the recovery programme was practical, personal and with an essential spiritual component.

The staff were and still are caring, professional, encouraging, understanding, non-judgemental, tough when necessary, and they have the ability to apply these attributes individually to each person. My mind was opened. The experience made me see that I had a part to play in my own recovery. It was not forced on me, it was a two way process. You cannot impose the truth by force, and coerced agreement is not consent.

The alcoholic, at certain times, has no effective mental defence against the first drink. The emotional damage done to those around you is bad enough, but the harm done to ourselves is greater. Very deep, sometimes quite forgotten damaging emotional conflicts persist below the level of consciousness. These feelings (all those drinks) can twist our personalities and alter our lives for the worse.

Thoughtful reflection and spirituality are my defence mechanisms now.

To place instincts first will drag me backwards into disillusionment and its deadly consequences. To place spiritual growth first means I have a real chance; the possibility – no, probability – of being happy and useful to all those lovely people around me.
God bless.

Name: Lily Brown
Age: 30
Condition: Anxiety, Post Traumatic Stress Disorder
Location: London, United Kingdom

Today, during my commute, my eyes got stuck. I was standing on the train to London Waterloo, and my eyes ran over the same phrase six or seven times. It was in the middle of an article, but these

A Day in My Head

particular words came adrift, like they'd been cut loose, and my interest in the rest dropped away.

All around me, people were trying not to touch each other in the crowded carriage. They were locking their legs into tight little coils under their seats, or pulling their shoulders in, and apologising when they didn't quite manage it. On bad days, I do something similar, except what I'm doing is trying not to let my insides touch my outsides.

For instance, when I read a paper, I'll often get the urge to cry. It's part of why I've stopped reading newspapers much. It's humiliating the way I can't stop myself from crying in public. Those human-interest stories – the dead girlfriends, the abused babies, the rape that happened round the corner – I hate that stuff. When people tell me not to cry during horror films because it's "made up", I think they're idiots. No depravity is "made up". Every single one of those eviscerations has happened, and when you watch them, you're watching something real.

We like seeing people's insides. A large amount of what we seek, what we click, what we consume, is about exposing what's hidden.

My body will do anything to stop my insides from coming out. It will send me into a full-blown fight-or-flight adrenalin crash rather than let that happen.

If they get out, I might get so angry I'd hit someone. If they get out, I might never be
myself again. I might not stop myself, next time I think of jumping off the balcony.

If I let them out, people would see them in my face, and they would know I'm not normal.

When I have a panic attack, my mind tries to stop my body from panicking, because a body in full panic feels like a mad body, a pathological body. But when my body panics, it's trying to stop something, too. It's trying to stop me feeling the things that, when I should have felt them, I couldn't: fear, pain, anger and despair.

It wasn't a conscious decision. Some part of me just wrapped them up and put them to one side, and I stepped out of myself, like a tenant vacating a room.

We all know the first stage is Denial. But they don't tell you that long after your mind has accepted something, your body holds fast to its wilful ignorance. I know what happened to me, but my body still refuses it. I don't know if I will ever mourn enough, rage enough, fall far enough, hurt enough, to convince my body that what happened is over. My body is still trying to preserve itself. It wants me to run, when it's far too late for running. It wants me to fight, when the possibility of resistance is long past.

The six words that caught my eye were, "Trauma is not pathology, but history".

My trauma was caused by a mundane act. I have all my limbs and digits; my face is unscathed. I know some people will envy me having something I can point to and say, "This is the cause." But history is not solid. The more I try to untangle what happened to me, the more I realise that things I thought were caused by it actually existed before, maybe even led me to it. The act has weight, it distorts history, makes itself seem unique, when in fact maybe it was part of a long series of cause and effect that has not yet reached its end.

Until my body stops replaying my rape over and over, trying to find the history that fits, I will have panic attacks. I don't know if they'll ever stop. If my body ever gives up the fight, I don't know what the consequences will be. But I know this: I can't say, "This part of me is sick, cut it out", because this sickness grows from a healthy root. There's a reason for its flowering. Either I keep cutting off the head, or I can wait for it to bear fruit.

Name: Melissa Sue Tucker
Age: 40
Condition: Brother's Addiction
Location: Arizona, United States

I've been thinking about my little brother a lot lately. I remember when I was 12 years old and he was only two years old, he used to run around in our backyard in only cowboy boots and a diaper. He was so cute, sweet, innocent. It's weird but I grew up feeling like he was mine. I wonder if I hadn't left home at 17, or if I'd taken him with me.... Would he be a homeless heroin addict who makes money by stealing from other people? I know I can't blame myself, but sometimes I do. I wish I could help him – somehow. I know he's 30 years old now and he is responsible for his own choices. But there's a part of me that still sees that innocent two year old whom I would do anything for.

A Day in My Head

When I think back over the last month or so, my heart just breaks. It breaks for my brother, my family, and for all the other "Daniels" out there. And of course, it breaks for all of their families.

———————

Monday April 18, 2016 morning:

My brother, 10 years my jr, was released from jail. Here we go again! Argh! At least when he's in jail I know he's safe. I know he has food and a roof over his head. I'm hopeful that he will do what he's supposed to do this time around. I hope that he takes advantage of the help available to him!

Tuesday April 19, 2016 afternoon:

I wanted to find out where my brother was so I messaged him on Facebook. I also called Pinal County Parole office, found out who his PO was and left him a voicemail.

Tuesday April 19, 2016 7:22pm:

He sent me this text:

Hey Sis, this is Daniel. Give me a call tomorrow or whenever you get a chance. I'm gonna be doing my parole here in Tucson. When I'm done I want to get in to some counselling and want to know if you know any psychologists that work or of the whole positive thinking thing...

Tuesday April 19, 2016 8:19pm:

OMG I feel so excited! Hopeful! I called him and we talked for one hour and three minutes.
We had a really great conversation. He told me that he knows I've always loved him and been there for him. He told me that every time I begged him to talk to me and tell me what was going on, he wanted to – he just did not know how. He told me that he's been reading the book we sent him and really liked it. He said he's been meditating. When he was in prison, he was diagnosed bipolar, borderline personality disorder, with suicidal tendencies. They put him on meds and he did not like how he felt. They tried something else and he did not like them either. He did not want to take meds, he wanted to figure out how to feel better naturally. We talked about how important nutrition is to feeling clear headed. He did not know that nutrition would have an impact so he asked

lots of questions about that. He said he'd been meditating and that was helping.

He said he remembers being six years old, walking to school and wishing he could wake up from this dream. He remembers ditching school in fourth grade. He would hide behind the fence until my mom went to work. I told him about the podcast I'm doing. I told him about Crossroads and the recovery community I've made friends with in Phoenix. He told me he wanted to come to Phoenix but had signed a 90 day contract with a halfway house in Tucson. He told me he did not want to stay in Tucson though, he did not like it there. We talked about the dangers of doing heroin, how fentanyl is killing people. He said that he doesn't want to die. He said he never used to nod out or pass out. He said he only likes to do enough to help him feel ok. He said any time he tried something new or used after not using for a while he only used a little bit to test it out. He sounded sober and clear-headed. He told me he doesn't feel like using. I told him I was really sorry for all the things I've said to him over the years. I told him I love him and want to have a relationship with him. No matter what happens, even if he does decide to use again, I still want to maintain a relationship with him. He told me he wants to have a relationship with me too. Even though he knows my mom loves him – he knows I've always loved him and been there for him too. I told him I'll come see him next week in Tucson. He said he should be able to leave the halfway house for a few hours when I come down.

Wednesday April 20, 2016 morning:

I texted him "Good Morning" and he texted "Morning, sis" that was the last time I heard from him. Later that day, his PO called me because Daniel hadn't checked in with him yet … and he hadn't checked into the halfway house that he was supposed to be at. I called Daniel and left a voicemail. I sent him a few texts.

My mom spoke to Daniel on Wednesday. He told my mom that we had a good conversation. That was the last time she heard from him.

Sunday April, 24, 2016:

I was in the shower and started freaking out about my brother. I heard him say "Don't worry about me sis, I'm happy now". Then I had a vision that his body was in a dumpster behind a Target in Tucson. I texted Daniel and my mom (after my shower) to find out what's going on. My mom said she hadn't heard from him and asked if I could talk. I called her and we are both in the same space. It sucks. He has a warrant out for his arrest because he has not checked in with his PO. His PO called all the halfway houses in Tucson and hasn't been able to find him. It seems like he just told us what we wanted to hear. I am left wondering if it was goodbye.

Not knowing is the hardest part…

Monday May 2, 2016:

My mom let me know she's heard from my brother. I'm so glad he's alive. He checked in with his PO and entered a 30 day rehab so that's really awesome news! I love him so much, I hope he can see his value!

Sunday May 9, 2016:

Mother's Day! My mom came over and we had an amazing day. She did tell me that she had heard from Daniel. He did not stay in the rehab and he has another warrant out for his arrest. I guess he's moved from Tucson back to Phoenix and is "living" in Glendale or somewhere on the west side. I don't know if there's a house where they can all just hang out and get high together, or if he lives at parks and bus stations. I can't even think about it because I get so mad at him. He has access to help and he just does not want it.

Name: Zalie Benda
Age: 49
Condition: Obsessive Compulsive Disorder
Location: London, United Kingdom

It came upon him like a demon in the night at just nine years old … the bully that is OCD. Wracked with fear and anxiety and asking me persistently if he had chocolate on his face. Was I sure he didn't … was I sure … was I sure ... was I sure! His lego had blown away hadn't it? Like magic just all blown out of the window and down the country lanes … hadn't it … had it? Had it? HAD IT? Inspecting his hands for specks, his shoes for flecks, had he touched the killer yew tree in the graveyard, had he been contaminated by the bin bag that we saw 50 yards off, the washing and washing and checking and washing, and what about the raw chicken? Never dismiss raw meat! But more than all of this, so much more, was the look of terror in his eyes. "Please help me," he said late one night as he clung to me in bed, heart racing, panic taking hold yet again. We had seen three top dogs by then … one tried to put tea on his hand, one said he was a very, very troubled boy and one was a regular Robin Williams … should have done stand up. Missed the boat there! I read everything I could find, I sat on the trampoline hidden in the bottom garden and wept, food tasted like nothing and I wasted quickly away. I wept more until all the wet had gone from my insides. I just wanted to TAKE IT AWAY. HAVE IT ALL MYSELF AND FOR THE SUN TO SHINE IN MY SON'S EYES.

He thought I might be an alien, you know, that life might be a dream. "Are you real, mum?" "Yes." "Are you sure?" "Yes." "How do I know you are not lying?" "You have to trust me on this." But he didn't. He hides behind his books at school grimacing as the panic took hold ... was the teacher real? Was she an alien too? "How many panics today?" I asked as casually as I could but wanting to vomit all the while ... only three today ... in science. If I touch the test tube in chemistry I could die. If I die I will go into the box of eternal darkness ... aware but trapped forever and ever. Aware but helpless. "That won't happen", I insist. "How come you know ... you've never even died!" I don't have the answers. Is this my fault? What did I eat during pregnancy ... was it the antibiotics? Is it in my genes ... did I do this to my boy? This is all my fault. I watch him sleep. It is the only time he is free from the demon; his lips swollen and relaxed, his limbs heavy, eyes motionless in their sockets. Perhaps tomorrow won't be so bad, please god, please god I'll do anything.

When the morning light wakes my son the first thing he does is check his hands for specks.

The demon is back.

Name: Emma Bryant
Age: 25
Condition: Post Traumatic Stress Disorder, Anxiety, Depression
Location: West Sussex, United Kingdom

I half-heartedly drag myself out of bed around 1pm to get ready to meet my friend who is coming over to spend the afternoon with me. She and I have recently both ended relationships with extremely abusive men, who have sucked 90% of our souls out of us. I struggled with insomnia last night, as I have done for the previous two months, due to panic attacks and a "chattering mind", so don't really feel like facing the day. It's sunny outside but I don't feel uplifted or happy, I feel just like I do every other day – miserable and anxious. Since I walked away from the man who was slowly killing me, I have felt a ridiculous range of emotions every single day – usually anger and despair. I should be happy that I have set myself free from a life of pain and degradation, however I feel I

A Day in My Head

have already lost everything, and don't see how I can build myself back up from this. I have recently been diagnosed with anxiety, depression and PTSD (Post Traumatic Stress Disorder), mostly due to the horrendous abuse I suffered at the hands of said emotionally and verbally abusive ex-partner, with whom I stayed for 18 months, wrongly believing I could "save" him and bring him happiness.

My friend arrives around 2pm and we immediately get started on our favourite activity – drinking three or more bottles of wine. We both know we have a problem, as we drink to try and forget our worries. I also know I shouldn't be drinking this heavily whilst on medication, but I am willing to risk that in order to feel some element of artificial happiness. I sign into my Facebook account and feel strong pangs of sadness and envy when I see photos of friends and work colleagues enjoying themselves on days/nights with their families and partners, as my family now won't talk to me due to my risky and sometimes aggressive behaviour (from back when I was in a relationship with my abuser, and also from when I would drink so much that I would forget where I was and who I was speaking to).

My friend then points out a "status" by a lady with whom I do not get along. It is very obviously about me – saying that I am deluded and reiterating claims by my ex-partner that we were, in fact, never in a relationship. She goes on to state that she "pities" me, and that her and my abuser have had a good laugh at how "confused" and "unstable" I must be to fabricate "an entire relationship from nowhere". I break down in tears and my friend comforts me. I know I have never done anything to hurt or offend this lady, and I am upset and confused as to why she feels the need to write this kind of thing. I scroll down through the "comments" section and read even more untrue and revolting things from two other females that I once deemed "friends" of mine. They state that I am a horrible and bitter person who "needs serious psychological help" – I know they copied this quote from my abuser, as he used to tell me this all the time, every time I would cry after he'd degraded me in public and called me names. My body goes into a state of shock and I feel bile rising in my throat. I know this is a mixture of the alcohol and my nerves/paranoia, but my mind is spinning. I run to the bathroom and proceed to vomit into the toilet. My friend is also angry as she knows I went through hell and back with that monster of a "man". We take another drink. She suggests we take a walk to the local bar, then remembers that I am barred from there, due to my ex starting a verbal fight with a member of staff some months ago. We open our second bottle of wine.

The afternoon mostly consists of me getting worked up, wondering how someone who was once my friend, and witnessed the abuse on more than one occasion, could spew such venom about me publicly for everyone to see. What also hurts is the fact that two other girls, whom I have never spoken badly of, are also jumping on the bandwagon and making revolting personal comments about me. My friend reminds me that in our line of work, these people are considered "nobodies" and "amateurs" whilst I am at the height of my career. I know she is right, and that there is clearly an element of jealousy to their remarks, but it still cuts deep, as I have always considered myself to be a kind, moralistic, hardworking and well respected individual.

Our "line of work" is fundamentally the adult entertainment industry from which I have been successfully transitioning away into the mainstream acting and comedy business – something which I have always longed to do. I have had an extremely successful career in the adult industry, working as a model for "top shelf" men's magazines, and also, for lack of a less graphic phrase, porn films. I find the majority of the people I work with to be mentally healthy individuals with a reasonable level of intelligence; however, unfortunately, on occasion you do inevitably encounter a person who initially seems like a respectable and sane individual, but ultimately turns out to be missing a few fries from their Happy Meal, so to speak. Not the full Shard.

Together we finish the second bottle of wine, and then it is the time of the evening that I have been dreading – time for my friend to leave my house for the day and go to pick up her daughter from school. I hate being alone in this big house so much, as time alone means time with my own thoughts. I have been feeling quite morbid and distorted the last few weeks, as though all the days are blending into one. I don't miss my ex, but I want answers. Why didn't he love me the way I thought I loved him? Why was he always angry with me? What did I do to make him hate me so much? My friend leaves and I go to the local store to buy another bottle of wine. I plan to drink until I feel tired as that is the only way I can fall asleep some nights.

I put my headphones in and listen to some music as this usually helps to liven me up a bit. I feel so sad that my friend is gone and wish she could come back so that I won't be alone. I picture her going back to her bright, happy home and her family. I wish I had somewhere I could go to escape from the walls of this house and all the bad memories they hold. I contemplate phoning my mum, then remember that she "doesn't feel ready" to talk to me after my

A Day in My Head

breakdown last Christmas when I was at the height of desperation (due to the state of my dismal relationship). I decide instead to take the plunge and call a domestic abuse helpline as I feel I want to talk to someone outside of my situation and who knows nothing about me and who therefore can't judge me. I end up crying and being rude to the lady who answers my call. I don't mean to be – I just struggle at the moment to get my words out and explain how I feel. The lady can tell I am obviously working myself up and tells me to calm down, but I can't and she ultimately terminates my phone call.

By now it is around 11am and I am starting to feel sleepy. I put a comedy DVD on the TV and end up falling asleep on my sofa in my dressing gown. I think the alcohol has had its desired effect as I sleep reasonably peacefully until midday the following afternoon.

Madly in Love

According to Dr. Tian Dayton, Clinical Psychologist and author; "it is love that gives a person a sense that they are worthy and valuable. It is love that motivates us to be more than we thought we could be, that gives us the courage to do something as mind-boggling as get married or have a child. Within love are all of those components that make us able to forge on in a world that is constantly offering up challenges to our sense of self."

The opposite of love is mental illness.

Name: Aron Bennett
Age: 30
Condition: Obsessive Compulsive Disorder
Location: Norwich, United Kingdom

"My Sweet Sertraline"

May 16th 1996

I am ten years old. This week we have been lumbered with a substitute teacher, Mr Baxter, who is bald and unfriendly and makes us do boring problem solving instead of literature and art. Mrs Willis, our usual teacher, is on honeymoon, which I hardly feel is appropriate, considering last week he (her unfledged bridegroom) definitely upset her and she was in a ferocious mood. How I know this is that I wanted her to see this poem I had written, see, about a giant inferno engulfing the earth (despite having read that between fire and ice, the world would surely end in ice) but she didn't seem the least bit interested. In fact, she wouldn't even look at me! And so I ended up just standing there, like a *schlemiel*, by her desk. All the while her head remained slumped into the beautiful creases of her recently bronzed, somewhat pileous elbows. Until all of a sudden, sensing my presence, she bolted upright and glared piercingly into my eyes, her downy lip now quivering with rage: "*What the.... Why are you just standing there!? Can't you see I'm in no mood you little ... "*

Nevertheless, Mrs Willis is still my favourite teacher. She taught me how to write and to this very day gives me copious team points on account of my advanced academic ability. I, for one, and certainly in my professional opinion, think she can do much better than her current husband.

May 16th 2004

A Day in My Head

Today I tell the girl I am infatuated with how I feel about her. My best friend Jake (shorter than me) has been encouraging me to say something for some time. This girl with beautifully burnished red hair and coffee eyes and pale skin and an ever so slightly disproportioned forehead. And so, guts tied up, dry mouthed, I express my feelings to her outside the school gates following a drink at the local pub, The Maid's Head. "I love you," I tell her sincerely, my heart oozing like Virgin Naphtha (how aptly titled) down to the end of my very best dolman sleeve. Horrified, she looks at me and tells me that she is fond of me before running off in floods of tears towards the school building, her beautifully burnished red hair flailing and glistening in the sunlight behind her.

She is fond of me. I am fond of Haimisha cucumbers. I will not ask out another girl so long as I live.

May 16th 2015

It's been a few years since I was last in compulsory education and I am all the better for it. At university I was diagnosed with OCD – partly caused by all the rejection from women, so my doctor said – and it has taken a while to get my act together. Today is my book signing; a memoir about OCD, which I am flogging at the local city forum for the generous price of £12.99. Loads of people come to see me, which is nice, though the one person I really want to show doesn't. Her name is Amber. We met five years back, selling mobile phones. She is extremely attractive, magnificent body, way out of my league, but we get on well. On Facebook, we can literally talk and laugh for hours at a time. I think we have a connection. My counsellor thinks I am an excellent shoulder to cry on.

Nevertheless, I have my writing. It is perhaps only when I contemplate chronicling the circadian madness, documenting the ludicrous and the farcical, does it all ever mean anything more to me than the series of pointless happenings and random dead ends that it no doubt must mean to everybody else. Writing about life, somehow, I am not quite sure how, seems instantly capable of transforming the hard and the prosaic into an abundance of delicious meaning, exploding with colour and excitement.

It also doesn't stamp all over your heart with a pair of PU synthetic, mid-cut *chaussures rigides.*

May 16th 2016

I am not in love. In fact, due to the medication (100mg of Sertraline), I am not even in lust. *Oh, my Sweet Sertraline.* Nonetheless, the prospect of never finding a partner and dying alone still makes me care enough to journey to the gym. I am actually in pretty good shape these days. On the way, I take a detour to my local Waterstones. I enter the biography section and, amidst titles by Dave Pelzer, Augusten Burroughs and *Morrissey*, it soon dawns on me just how unremarkable my life has become. I am normal and healthy and finally thinking clearly.

I rather like being normal.

I pick out a few titles to read; one of them is a diary by Lena Mukhina. It looks harrowing. It's about a girl's life during the Siege of Leningrad. One minute a teenager, worrying about homework and contemplating unrequited love and the next …

Who was it that said that between fire and ice, the world would end in ice?

Name: Hannah Grant
Age: 22
Condition: Borderline Personality Disorder
Location: Diss, Norfolk, United Kingdom

Bought a cat today. She's cute, pretty and I've named her Hope. I'll be collecting her this coming Wednesday. Why is this relevant? I'm currently lying in bed trying to decide whether this is my way of distracting myself from the recent end of a relationship, or whether this is my BPD, cushioning my grief with powerful impulsive behaviours. Previous purchases include a MacBook Air, a finance deal on a Kia Rio, and a £300 handbag. All directly caused by relationships ending or general emotional upset. This entry couldn't have come at a better time. Today I truly evaluated the impact my disorder has on my life, and how much I can control it. In the recent weeks past I was on the wine at the stroke of 8pm every night after mothering duty had finished. I would drink myself into oblivion, track down my then boyfriend and proceed to either be wildly loving with him, or rip him to shreds in an argument. There was no in-between. No "I'm off to sleep, goodnight". Needless to say, he's gone now. Today, after the final arrangements with the lady selling Hope, I thought to myself, "Is this me or my BPD?" This time last year, if I went through anything remotely emotionally painful, a tidal wave of rage, suicidal fantasies and fear would sweep through me. I'd be carried off by my out of control and terrifyingly out of proportion reactions. My way of coping would be to bring loved ones down with me. I would scream, smash my head against walls (even when eight months pregnant) drive off and transfer all my money to my parents and tell them this was the end. Incredibly dark times indeed. With several bumps along the way

A Day in My Head

(psychological breakdowns in my world), I have managed to get a grip. Since all my flaws were put to me by my best friend of the last three years, who washed his hands and said "no more", I was left asking myself how much longer will I let this go on? So I bought a self help book, I haven't touched a drop of booze despite the fruity bottles of forget me juice constantly calling me. Now, by no means am I saying all is peachy. There are more wild outbursts to come, more sitting truly debating whether a knife to the jugular would be the best solution to an everyday issue. But today I decided, I'm truly going to give it a shot. To be me, not my BPD. And also the best goddamn cat owner you've ever seen.

Name: Melanie Anne Ball
Age: 25
Condition: Personality Disorder
Location: London, United Kingdom
Profession: External Training Officer at Rethink Mental Illness, Lecturer at Canterbury Christ Church University and Cofounder & Playwright at Heart to Heart Theatre

Dear Miss Stephens,

You
showed me
surrogacy isn't
just for birth
not that
it's about
better
or worse
because there's no script-
no chapter
or verse
that anyone could quote
that could've helped
with all the
behaviour
mumbling words
thrown chairs
and low attendance
that was in
the whirlwind
that I turned up with.
Parenting
is a multidisciplinary team

Aron Bennett

and you
gave me
an earth
to plant my feet on
and get my teeth into.
My home
for those months
was you
and your art room
with all the turp fumes
and the year nines giggling
at the
"fuck you"
that in adolescent grief
I had stitched onto
that duvet.
An over attached pupil
who cried in every lesson
and couldn't stay still
grew up
and learned how to feel
something
that looks okay.
Yet still
you sit in my mind
as a symbol
of what was once
still beating.
In my chest.
Dear Miss,
you showed me all of this:
how to shade
how to paint
how to mix
the colours I couldn't see
or feel
didn't matter that the room
felt unreal
lying dormant
in another day
the head of year shouting
the sewing machine breaking
the weeks disappearing
the other girls sneering
at the clichés
I was making

A Day in My Head

in my "artwork".
Just get something on the canvas
It will talk
It will say
something
to us.
Expression isn't about
getting it right
not turning up
for the fight
but noting a presence
even late
past submission date
is okay
because when you said to me
You can do it, Melanie!
I believed you
enough to try
and make it come true.
I wrote you a letter
do you remember?
It said nothing I needed to
but I just wanted you
to know
that I still think of you
helping me to try
and have a go
at everything
that felt impossible.
So thank you
for teaching me
how to do it
with paint
chalk
dribbly ink
charcoal
you
sometimes felt like
the only one listening
and actually getting it.

My art teacher showed me how to finger-paint the faces of my
demons nose to nose and touch the tips of angels' wings with my
paintbrush. I never would have made it to where I am today without
her.

But I wouldn't have made it to today without the struggle along my mental health journey either.

My experiences with my mental health have been horrific. I have been mad, bad and sad. I have been tormented, exhausted, hopeless and helpless.

But what I am grateful to know today is this: my insatiable hunger for the life, my love for other human beings, and the compulsion I feel to fight for a better world has been powered by every day I have ever spent feeling like my head was going to explode. Every crippling moment of terror and every gut wrenching, agonising wave of despair is worth it. And yes, that is easier to say on the good days – of course.

But on the darkest days, where I could read back what I have written and just hear a smug liar, striving for unattainable victory over the beast, I must return to this:

Everyone wants happiness
and nobody wants pain
but you can't have a rainbow
without a little rain.

Today, just for today, I'm grateful for both rain and rainbows. And people like Miss Stephens, who open their hearts to give you some shelter when it's really pouring down.

Name: Ian D Bear
Age: 32
Condition: Gender Identity Dysphoria, Anxiety, Social Anxiety, Asperger's
Location: Norfolk, United Kingdom

Let me introduce myself. I am a transgendered man with a side of anxiety, social anxiety, depression, lingering agoraphobia and suspected Asperger's, along with some severe physical ailments.

Today was a difficult day. I spent the whole day out of my home comfort zone. I also did this with minus energy levels. I was pretty much misgendered the entire day. I am a man. I am a bald headed, bearded, overly-hairy manly man. But today I was referred to as 'she', 'her' and inclusively grouped amongst 'girls'. I am sure anyone who knows their gender identity would find it confusing to be referred to as the opposite gender. On top of that confusion, for

A Day in My Head

me it fills me with self doubt. It makes me question things: do I look female? Will I ever be thought of as one of the guys? Am I not manly enough? What am I doing wrong within my gender? – It was exhausting to say the least.

When I finally got home today I wanted to crash. I just needed to sleep, or to shut my mind off in front of the television. I've had a long distance relationship with my fiancée for three and a half years. When we're not together physically we communicate through the internet. My fiancée suffers from mental health problems quite severely, including paranoia and agoraphobia. This whole day I have been away from home, she has been alone. For her, she excitedly awaits me to get home for company. I am stuck between a rock and a hard place; her suffering or my suffering? I am, of course, going to choose to suffer. If I don't get online ASAP she will phone me, wondering where I am. Her paranoia will kick in. She will be worried in case something has happened to me. The phone! Another of my anxieties. The mere sound of it ringing makes my heart palpitate. Most people in my life ignore my request to not be phoned.

I did get online straight away, only to be met by social media full of belittling commentary over the seriousness of trans toilet rights. Bees dying is more important than worrying about toilet usage rights in America apparently … but trans humans are being beaten, raped and murdered!? I found myself in dialogue with a hateful American. I was bullied. I was called Mrs Doubtfire, Ian Jenner and Ru Paul. I was told that my views infringe on the basic rights of citizens in that country. I was told that trans people are bringing this hatred on themselves by forcing others to agree. I was mocked about my profile picture – a loving photo of myself and my fiancée. Here comes more self-doubt, already fuelled by today's misgendering. The pain my heart felt was indescribable and I felt a heavy disappointment in humanity. Today I have not been accepted by the world. I feel blessed though that my fiancée was there, metaphorically holding my hand through it all, supporting me and the trans community. I got online for her when I was exhausted. It ended up with her being there for me.

I love my fiancée. It is very tough, two people with mental health problems being in a relationship. We work very hard to be good to each other. Even though we suffer mentally, we are psychologically mature with each other. We are an honest and truthful couple. For me, the hardest thing is her paranoia. Her biggest fears fuel her paranoia. One of her biggest fears is losing me. It becomes a vicious circle; my social anxiety and her paranoia. She is paranoid I will be looking at other females when we're out. I am anxious when I'm out, but now doubly anxious that my eyes will go in the wrong direction innocently, but to her my eye direction is suspicious. I am a good man, I know this, and she knows this, but mental health kicks both our arses at times. It's not a question of trust, it's a question of brain dysfunction on both our parts. My paranoia of her paranoia is worse than the reality of her paranoia. She's barely paranoid about me when we're out. I'm very paranoid that she's paranoid. She does have professional mental health support. I do need and want to find out if there's support for partners affected mentally by the mental health problems of their partner. If you see what I mean...

Name: Shelley Erswell
Age: 36
Condition: Psychosis
Location: Cleethorpes, United Kingdom
In a Relationship with: Ian D Bear

It's 9:00am and, as if robotically by now, I am about to take my handful of medications. I, of course dislike, this part intensely. The pills are overly large, chalky; they make me gag and choke, regurgitating them in my mouth before being able to swallow them down. It's all yuck but the alternative is to experience psychotic episodes. So I swallow the pills, begrudgingly, everyday.

Today is a difficult day; as a reclusive, introverted, hermit, and with an impending appointment with my doctor, I have to battle the anxiety of facing the 'outside world'. I can feel the tension in my veins, the heart beating faster, the layer of sweat on my palms, the tremors of my hands, the dizzying feeling in my head. I conjure myself to make it out of my house. Just. It is inside the building with 'other humans' that concerns me, being in such close proximity to other people. Their being able to see me. Watch me as I sit there in a state of panic. Knowing that they take their mental health for granted. Knowing that I can rely upon my mental un-health to make me look like a dysfunctional human to the mass populous. It's all terribly draining.

For me, 'normal' is having my senses overwhelmed by the outside world. After 16 years of reclusive living, the world beyond my front door is a 'fairground'. Bright lights. A cacophony of loud noise. Vehicles whizzing by. Strong smells in the air. My senses are literally flooded by so many sensations that it can leave me cowering in pain, rocking and covering my ears, closing my eyes

A Day in My Head

tightly, and willing myself to be back indoors, back inside my 'safe place'. Episodes like this happen less these days; my senses are gradually being exposed to the world again and my symptoms are lessening. Still, it has been a test of endurance just to step outside on any given day.

Lately I have been suffering an increase in paranoid thinking, so I'm to discuss these issues. It may be that I require an increase in medication. I am currently receiving Cognitive Behavioural Therapy to help with my sporadic thinking and lack of self control in any area of my life. My psychiatrist and I are hoping that these things will help me function in daily life.

Of course, I am also missing my love. I grieve and pine when I am not with him. We presently live and love long distance. We met online in a forum three and a half years ago, went on to meet up in real life, dated, and have been in love madly ever since. He has been good for me. So good.

He completely 'gets' my mental un-health. He is supportive and encourages me to go to those therapy appointments. It was very early days in our romance – three years ago –
when I suffered a psychotic breakdown. He loved me through it though, and was immensely supportive as the team of mental health workers/nurses/full time live-in carers entered my life to care for me.

My life changed but his love for me never did.

We have an honest relationship where we can each opine freely. We have shared all and everything with each other, including our states of mental un-health. I suffer psychosis, depression, severe anxiety and agoraphobia. He has experience of agoraphobia and currently suffers depression and social anxieties.

We just 'get' each other.

We're about to finally make the move to live together. He had expressed that he wishes for me to be 'weller' when we live together. He needs his partner to be his equal, to have equal responsibilities of running and caring for the home. He is anxious about being moulded into the role of my 'carer,' but as neither of us want that for him, I am striving to help myself become more functional after 16 years of being a dysfunctional recluse. I have assured him that I will do my all, including therapy sessions to learn how to function in society, so that I will be his equal while living together.

So far, so good!

I am learning coping skills, ways to deal with anxiety. How to recognise and reconcile my paranoia. I feel positive. Absolutely. I now feel that I can become a functioning adult female who can live a full life of love, adventure and joy!

Name: Aron Bennett
Age: 30
Condition: Obsessive Compulsive Disorder
Location: Norwich, United Kingdom

Of course, I have not always been a contented singleton. Oh no, no, no. Once upon a time, I might well have fixated over the old Lennon-McCartney shibboleth: "All you need is love". Now that pithy maxim seems like a somewhat mawkish assertion that life might be purposeless if devoid of tenderness and devotion – without intrigue and *amore*.

My own Bildungsroman, should I ever wish to start one, would no doubt chronicle, both synoptically but also in closer detail, my fascination, my obsession and, ultimately, my disappointment with this one, uncompounded pursuit which, over the years, has both fed and assuaged my mental ill health. Love was important to me because I felt like it had always been withheld. Though now, of course, when I look back at this failed endeavour to meet The One, I have the choice to appraise it within a purlieu of what is now fashionable, the current *dernier cri*. Or rather, the lens of postmodernity, in which people no longer seek love; they are not in search of a partner but just another warm body, a steaming carcass to wake alongside, to kiss and to grope goodbye before crisply and callously blocking them on social media. Single again, but only until the next sinistral *swipe*. Or is it a swipe to the right?

I am as much a victim of this culture as a perpetrator. I am single because no one is good enough for me and *I* am not good enough for anybody. An endless merry-go-round. Much like mental illness.

As I stand in Waterstones still perusing the titles, I remember a time when this was not so. I was 18-years-old and my best friend Jake and I had decided to each buy a copy of Martin Amis' *The Rachel Papers*. It was our first joint-trip to this magnificent tome-packed stadium, just opposite the medieval castle. Both infatuated with a girl at the time - not the *same* girl - we read this book to indulge our lascivious expectancies. Virginal and

A Day in My Head

naive, we clung to Amis' mechanical, blow-by-blow (literally) accounts of coition between the reedy protagonist with whom we could both relate, and the tender though vacuous heroine, Rachel. Unfortunately for both of us, it would be a lot later before either of us would gain a true taste of intimacy.

For me, my first experience of love – *Le coup de foudre* – was of the unreturned variety and thus had little to do with sex and frivolity. Or even true love. Instead, the relationship remained largely in my own head. A clue perhaps? A hint of things to come? For whilst I could not be said to have been *in love*, I was no doubt love *sick*. Not surprisingly, the second book I bought from my local Waterstones, aged 19 this time, was the eponymously titled volume by renowned psychologist and lecturer, Frank Tallis. "Love sickness," writes Tallis, "has very similar consequences to mental illness. Clearly, a 'clinically significant' amount of distress and general impairment are an almost inescapable consequence of falling in love."

It is perhaps no surprise that the inescapable consequences of my own unrequited love would be the commencement of a whole rafter of obsessional tendencies, categorised latterly as OCD. And as with the intrusive thoughts that ensued, my unwillingness to move on from the object of my unseemly affection – our coalescence having long ceased to be a viable proposition – became, ultimately, a thankless pursuit, which would lead not only to suffering and angst but also to total extirpation, like a collapse of an otherwise burgeoning universe into totally dimensionless singularity.

A few years later, aged 21, I met another girl. It was a rather brief affair. She worked in the cafe in the Morrisons store where I was also working at the time as a checkout operator. She was attractive, sassy, with a long black Morrison's pencil skirt which dropped down passed her knees like she had just stepped out of Edwardian Britain, and the two of us ended up in bed after only two weeks of dating. Though, when it came to it, I had been somewhat short of *potent* ...

Now when I look back at those so-called halcyon days, I laugh to myself. Rejection, the occasional diminutive performance, the risk of sexually transmitted infections and more generally, *une incertitude de jeunesse*; romantic relationships have proven, in their limited way, only to enhance my own experiences of anxiety. Colossal anxiety. No more successful with women these days, I have at least learned to adapt to the inevitable and mutual transposition of sexual desirability. Friend zones have been grudgingly met, at least at first, with platonic though nevertheless differential investment. Which is by no means entirely without benefit ...

Katrina, one of my best friends, is delightful and wise and a brilliant confidant; Keelia is like my caring, insightful, though 'officious' older sister; Emma is sarcastic and buxom and tells me she loves me almost as many times as my nan. Whilst the *ravissant* Ann-Marie, a patronymic match, is like my 'l'il sis'. Girls provide the best reassurance. They are also much better equipped at assuaging so much of my often very *personal* Obsessive-Compulsive symptomatology. The dyadic, or otherwise intimate nature of the 'fairer' endeavours for interpersonal maintenance are, without doubt, befitting for the more neurotic of the male species.

I am loved. And I love. Many women. Many *beautiful* women. And yet ... and yet, why is that I still feel so anxious. Just so ... *lonely* ...

A Day in My Head

Stigma

The second opposite of love …

Name: Tommy Dunne
Age: 58
Condition: Alzhemier's
Location: Liverpool, United Kingdom

Since I was diagnosed with Alzheimer's I've realised that once you tell people you have dementia you become invisible. People will talk about you, around you, over you but never *to* you. I'm tired of people coming up to my wife and asking how I am while I'm there; they will say to her, "Oh, it must be so hard for you, I don't know how you cope ..."

Recently, I was surprised when someone said to me: "Oh, my mum hasn't got dementia, she's got Alzheimer's". I tried to explain to them that if they think of all the makes of car there are, they still all sit under the umbrella of 'cars' and that, in the same way, there are over one hundred different forms of dementia, whereby Alzheimer's is simply another type; not different or separate at all.

Today on the bus I sat in one of the disabled seats, a man and a woman sitting either side of me. Unexpectedly, the man to my left turned to me and said: "Excuse me, you can't sit there." I said, "Why not?" He said, "They're for disabled people." I said, "I *am* disabled." He said, "You don't look disabled." I said, "You don't look stupid."

Then later on, at a group meeting, I watched as carers talked only to each other, while my peers were left out of the conversations entirely. When will people wake up to the idea that *conversation* is a process of 'give & take', absolutely essential in enabling my peers to retain a sense of themselves as well as, more generally, in facilitating participation. Over time I've noticed that the people I know with dementia are starting fewer and fewer conversations. This is very sad indeed. Moreover, I cannot help but observe how every time one is made aware that you have dementia they *always* avoid making eye contact with you. It's the same for my peers. This isn't good enough either. We *need* that eye contact; after all about 97% of communication is nonverbal.

If there's one thing I wish desperately to get across then it is this: let a person with dementia speak for themselves during discussions about their welfare or health issues. It is of vital importance. They may not speak up for themselves in other situations.

I find it infuriating that people think that once you have been diagnosed with dementia you lose your intelligence; nothing could be further from the truth. People with dementia still retain their brainpower.

I told a group today about the power of music. People should never underestimate the virtues of music as a relatively non-invasive and cost-effective intervention in the treatment and care of dementia. Music heightens our sense of identity and independence, improves our present mood, improves our awareness, improves our ability to understand and think. Life events are frequently accompanied by music. It makes intuitive, not to mention *rational*, sense that hearing music recalls life experience and emotion.

The sad thing about dementia is it will touch everyone one day, be it a grandparent, parent, spouse, relative, friend or neighbour; it will come calling, and there is no escaping it because it doesn't matter whether you're rich or poor, or what race or creed you are – the one thing about dementia is it doesn't discriminate.

While I have to try twice as hard every day to get through the day, I know it is worse for my wife because when I go to sleep I can have a break from it, whereas my wife has to live with it 24 hours a day, for I know she does not sleep well, worrying about me.

I know that I will not live to see a world without dementia, but I hope to live to see one that accepts it.

Name: Paras Yaseen
Age: 26
Location: Karachi, Pakistan
Profession: Doctor

I belong to a developing country in which talking about psychiatric disorders is considered a taboo. When I decided to be a psychiatrist, not a single person welcomed my decision. In fact, I remember a friend of my father coming to visit us at our home and when she asked what subject I was going to study and I said psychiatry she laughed out loud. Followed by something – I forget now the words - which was very disturbing to me. And so it was a tough decision even to choose psychiatry as my specialty. Stigma of psychiatric disorders is a major problem in the developing countries. As a result, most of the people remain untreated or undiagnosed, which causes distress, dysfunction and disability in the community. A collaborative report between the World Health Organization, World Bank, and Harvard School of Public Health revealed that while not

A Day in My Head

typically fatal, depression is the leading cause of disability worldwide.[1]

According to the statistics that are presented by WHO, globally, an estimated 350 million people of all ages suffer from depression, most of which are women. Fewer than half of those affected in the world (in many countries, fewer than 10%) receive treatment. But this is not even the worst of it. Depression is also a leading cause of suicide, which is the second leading cause of death in 15-29-year-olds.[2]

The National Institute of Mental Health defines depression as a serious but common illness characterized by prolonged periods of sadness that interfere with, or at worst, wreck daily life.[3] A person is diagnosed with depression if he presents with either symptoms of a depressed mood or loss of interest and pleasure, along with four other symptoms, such as changes in weight, changes in sleeping patterns, fatigue, feelings of worthlessness, or suicidal thoughts.[4] Depending on the number and severity of symptoms, a depressive episode can be categorized as mild, moderate, or severe. If left untreated, depression can be chronic, with frequent relapses. Of course, one must also remember that there are many different clinical pictures of depression, such as recurrent depressive episodes, bipolar affective disorder, or seasonal affective disorder.

Fortunately, we are born in the age in which many therapies for depression have been identified and are highly effective. For mild to moderate depression, psychotherapies such as Cognitive Behavioural Therapy and interpersonal therapy are very effective. These therapies enable the person to cope with the symptoms by teaching positive thinking strategies. For more severe cases, medications are used along with the psychotherapies, such as selective serotonin reuptake inhibitors (SSRI), serotonin and norepinephrine reuptake inhibitors (SNRI), monoamine oxidase inhibitors (MAO), and tricyclics.[3] Also, some brain stimulation therapies such as electroconvulsive therapy can be effective. Personally, I think making our bond stronger with God is the most effective therapy of all.

But regardless of the method, all these treatments can only be applied when patients have a true awareness and acceptance of his or her psychiatric condition. We need to understand that visiting a psychiatrist is not a sign of weakness, but indeed one of strength. We must also respect people who are going through some psychiatric issues as they need our love and support more than ever before. I want to say to everyone who is suffering with their mental health or even thinking of ending his or her life, "Please don't do this. You are loved. Talk to me or anyone near you but please don't do this to yourself and to us. We need you. This world needs you. If you are unhappy with anything, make that thing better for you and for the world so that no one can ever find any reason to be sad. Make this world a better place to live. But please don't fight this battle alone and don't say goodbye. Please."

REFERENCES:

1. Murray, C. J., A. D. Lopez, and D. T. Jamison. (1994). The Global Burden of Disease in 1990: Summary Results, Sensitivity Analysis and Future Directions. Bull World Health Organ 72(3), 495-509.
2. Depression:Fact sheet(2016). Retrieved from: http://www.who.int/mediacentre/factsheets/fs369/en/
3. Depression. (n.d.) National Institute of Mental Health. Retrieved from:
http://www.nimh.nih.gov/health/topics/depression/index.shtml#part 6.
4. Criteria for Major Depressive Episode: DSM-5. (n.d.) National Alliance for Mental Illness. Retrieved from:
http://www.nami.org/Content/NavigationMenu/Intranet/Homefront/Criteria_Major_D_Episode.pdf.

Name: Cathy Clarke
Age: 47
Condition: Obsessive Compulsive Disorder
Location: Greater Manchester, United Kingdom

Who Am I?

Do you really know who I am?

Am I a logo on a blog or a tweet on a Twitter feed?

Do I sit starkly amongst the other anonymous accounts that you have collated over the years?

Would you be able to pick me out in a line-up?

I thought not, because I have chosen to remain anonymous.

A Day in My Head

Female writers have been doing this for centuries. Two of my favourite novels were written by sisters under pseudonyms; they knew that if they were to reveal their true identities, no one would take them seriously because of their gender.

Have you heard of Currer and Ellis Bell? Possibly not. But I am certain that you will know them by their real names: Charlotte and Emily Brontë. Writing under pen names they produced *Jane Eyre* and *Wuthering Heights*, two of the greatest novels of all time.

Charlotte Brontë might not have been able to voice her opinions as a woman, but there was no holding back her heroine Jane Eyre:

"I am no bird; and no net ensnares me: I am a free human being with an independent will."

I am not a bird either. I am wilful and independent, but I am trapped. My trap is called stigma. However, unlike Jane, my net, the internet, has given me a voice.

Recently, PSHE programmes on Mental Health have been released to all schools in the UK. Wonderful people, such as Pooky Knightsmith, have worked tirelessly to ensure that teaching about Mental Health is made a priority in education. Yet this teacher still blogs anonymously. Why? OCD is misunderstood and its impact underestimated. I have felt the thorns of stigma first hand.

So, in a brave move, I'm writing under my real name for the first time. I hope that in time others will join me. Otherwise we will carry on perpetuating the stigma ourselves. I am not ashamed of having OCD, I'm just wary of your reaction when you speak to me about it.

Cathy Clarke aka @caughtinaloop

Name: Tricia Murray
Age: 38
Condition: Depression, Postnatal Depression
Location: Edinburgh, United Kingdom
Profession: Doula, EFT Practitioner, Perinatal Mental Health Campaigner

Today marks the start of Mental Health Awareness Week. Whenever I see large scale awareness-raising events for mental health, especially *perinatal* mental health, I feel a massive sense of pride. Proud that I'm part of a community of strong mums and dads, supporting each other and together fighting the stigma of perinatal mental ill health, which covers the period from conception all the way up until our babies are two, such manifestations including: antenatal/postnatal depression, maternal anxiety, maternal OCD, puerperal psychosis and 'baby blues'. I was diagnosed with PND when my youngest was nine months old – that's almost five years ago now and ever since, I've lived with the shadow of PND ...

I am part of a tribe of warrior women. I feel proud of my journey. At times, in an unexpected way, I'm even grateful to my illness for introducing me to my tribe and making me a stronger, better, kinder person. Right at this moment in time, today, 16th May 2016, I am well. Really well. It feels good. Life feels good.

Yet, not long ago, at the end of last year (2015), I could feel my mental health dipping. The warning signs came back – insomnia, inertia, feeling overwhelmed, the tears, the aches and pains in my body, my hair falling out (if you look closely you can see all my new hairs growing back).

This time when it happened, it came as a shock as I'd been so well. I felt myself panic. Panic that I was going to spiral into another deep depression. I became obsessed with keeping myself well – to the point that that in itself was exhausting, as it became my full time job – I couldn't stop researching anything and everything I could to keep the illness at bay. All day, all night, looking at therapies, supplements, herbs, anything that could possibly help. This time though, I had my tribe. People locally and nationally who I could speak to and who were in a position to help me and make space and time for me. This time, I managed to get better through self-care and the belief that, yes, I *could* get better and using strategies that I'd learned, including yoga, reducing alcohol and eating well. I'd also recently trained in EFT (Emotional Freedom Technique) and that really helped me too – regularly tapping on my physical and emotional state, which included some sessions with a local practitioner to work through the bigger stuff.

I call each dip in my mental health another cycle, as I find coming to terms with the fact that I have these cycles of my mental well-being a helpful way to view this. They are a signal to me that I need to re-prioritise my life. I'm recognising that I have yearly cycles and thereby also aware that every year at the start of winter, it's often the start of a new cycle. This year, I am clear I won't take on clients in December. That I will prioritise myself. That I will take every opportunity to self-care. I've come to recognise why self-care is so important; when I don't take that opportunity to look after myself, I can't be the mum/wife/daughter/sister/friend/doula that I want to be.

Something I find positive about living with the shadow of a mental health illness, is that every time I go through a cycle or episode, I learn a little bit more about myself. I learn how to heal the past and I gain strength. I grow stronger. I truly believe that a lot of this is being part of a community where I can acknowledge what is happening, where I can be vulnerable, where I can be honest, and where I can get support through people making the space to connect with me.

My only piece of advice to any person with a mental health condition is to connect to your tribe. In Edinburgh, if you are going through a perinatal mental health illness, then get in touch with Juno (www.juno.uk.com) which provides valuable local peer support. Anyone anywhere in the world can connect with the #PNDFamily on twitter (go to www.pndandme.co.uk for details).

Love and strength, Tricia xx

Name: Fiona J Stirling
Age: 28
Location: Scotland, United Kingdom

The Dutch Termination of Life on Request and Assisted Suicide Act (2002) requires that a patient's suffering be considered UNBEARABLE and HOPELESS for euthanasia to be legal.

This month, a woman was granted her request for a professionally assisted suicide due to persistently UNBEARABLE and HOPELESS mental health.

Her mind inflicted so much pain, it was considered she was in the same UNBEARABLE and HOPELESS condition as those suffering from terminal cancer, degenerative diseases, and severe physical disability.

Officially then - medically and legally - mental health has been recognised as just as crippling as a physical illness, which can actually take your arms, legs, and organs; as insidious as cancer; as painful as nerves on fire.

So ...

Perhaps, I'm only living because therapy keeps the chaos in remission.

Perhaps, the regular selective serotonin reuptake inhibitors dull the ache.

Perhaps, it's only HOPE keeping my own mind BEARABLE.

Name: Margaret Rose (Mary) Collins
Age: 25
Condition: Depression, Fibrous Dysplasia
Location: Cork, Ireland

I never know how to start things like this. "Hello, my name is Mary," I guess? You should probably also know that I have two chronic pain conditions: the first is fibrous dysplasia, which is a bone malformation (not always painful; I just got lucky!) The second is more enigmatic. You see, being stuck with chronic physical pain also led me to develop depression, a mental disorder that causes my brain to occasionally decide to fuck up my hormones.

When people find out I was once depressed, they always look at me differently. It's a bit like having a death in the family; everyone immediately looks at you with pity. Now you're "broken", they don't know what to say so they tell you how sorry they are… Except that with depression there is an extra twist of the knife; they probably believe that you're making at least some of it up.

That's the trouble with invisible disabilities – if seeing is believing, then you must be a fraud. It's hard to explain that I'm not lying. Unfortunately depression is very real.

It's a bit like having an emotional migraine - it hurts so badly that you cannot see and your very perception is skewed. Some days, it's a low hum that you can ignore; other days, it screams so loudly all you can do is huddle in a ball and sob until it calms down. It tends to be cyclical - you can go months with the low hum barely there at all, or else the screaming has been so loud for so long you don't remember what it is to not be in agony.

Today was a good day.

A Day in My Head

It has been a long few months. Changing career direction and being thrown in at the deep end was tough, in addition to dealing with physical illness and recovering from an unpleasant relationship. I'm also coming to terms with my current limitations. Depression ruins your cognition, you see. Your memory, your ability to retain and process information, to make decisions - it all goes to hell. People used to think it resolved with the rest of the symptoms, but researchers now believe that most depressed people are left with a permanent cognitive deficit.

I used to be brilliant. I could read something once and recite it word for word weeks later. I could see solutions others couldn't. I could do anything. Now? Every college assignment is late, not because I am depressed anymore, but because my brain refuses to click back into gear. Everything takes so much longer than it used to and it will probably never recover.

Today I thought back to when I was really depressed a few years ago. I believed that if I did everything I was supposed to (gym, counselling, medication, CBT, mindfulness, occupational therapy, to name a few things I've tried), that I would recover. I would be "me" again. I didn't realise that the person I was before all this is gone and she's never coming back. That's really hard to admit.

Today I snapped while talking to some old friends. Instead of arguing, as we often do, we ended up opening up to each other in ways we hadn't in a very long time. We embraced in tears. They told me I was loved. That I had shut down and cut everyone out but that I didn't have to do everything alone if I didn't want to. They were absolutely right.

That's one of the worst parts of depression; it makes you feel utterly alone. In reality, one in five people are depressed too. Most of my friends have had brushes with it in the past, which makes for a very empathetic support group. I'm very lucky in that regard; I have supportive friends and amazing family, even if I don't always remember they're there. The low hum is still in the background but I feel so much better. These are the moments you live for, the ones that give you hope.

It's ok if you never really recover - most people don't. Sometimes I'm so heartbroken that I'll never be that young girl again with a glittering future ahead, but then I remember how far I've come in my recovery, in my general life and I'm glad. It broke me down to nothing but I'm a stronger, better person because of it... and that's enough.

Name: Anita Levesque
Age: 42
Condition: Post Traumatic Stress Disorder
Location: Hamilton, Ontario, United States

Although I'm in Canada, today is the start of National Mental Health Awareness week in the UK and I'll be spreading the awareness. Mental health is a very important issue, and more so for me as I have had and have loved ones who live with mental illness. The stigma towards mental ill health is large, and since I became a mental health advocate in 2015 I am seeing more and more people opening up and talking about their mental illness.

My whole family is living with mental illness; my father lived with bipolar (I knew it as manic depression) all his life. When he passed away in 2004, my brother was diagnosed with PTSD, depression and anxiety; my mother and I now live with PTSD, as a result largely of living with violent domestic abuse, courtesy of my father's bipolar and prescription medication addiction. As you can see, mental illness is in very much a *family matter*.

Over the years my brother and I would spend every weekend at my grandmother's house. I always used to wonder why, although we always had a great time. Nevertheless, something never felt right. Years later, my mother explained to my why this was; she was protecting us.
I don't know how many times my father had attempted suicide; he tried strangling himself with belts and ties, tried drowning himself in the hot tub, even terrified us when he tried to shoot himself. There were many times where he would overdose into unconsciousness and the ambulance would be called.

Nevertheless, through everything, my father and I had a very special bond. Everyone would be sleeping, except him; he would wake me up and we would sit at the kitchen table and he would talk to me for hours, I would listen. I'm the only one he talked to like this, but I know it helped and he felt a bit better for it. As for me, it really hurt me to see him like this. Sure, we had our ups and downs, fought as normal father and daughter, over boys, me wanting a life, etc., but we were very close.

It has been 11 years since he passed and there's not a day that goes by I don't think of him. I think of the fights we had and look back at things differently now. Even though he had manic depression and the addiction, he was the best father anyone could ask for. He did provide for us, care about us and I know we meant the world to him.

A Day in My Head

In 2013, my boyfriend and I met for the first time, after knowing each other for three years prior. What I didn't know was that he too was living with mental illness; clinical depression, OCD, generalized anxiety disorder and a few personality disorders. After living with my father, knowing I had some tools at my disposal, I knew I could help my boyfriend and be a good support for him. We would communicate through text every day, I would help him through panic attacks, ease his depression somewhat. In a nutshell, I was just there for him; he told me his deepest darkest secrets. The day he moved in the reality hit. I saw, first hand, the affects of living with mental illness without medication (my father was on medication so there were no effects, except for overdoses).

While off his medication, it was like living in a nightmare. There were panic attacks, severe paranoia and fear, social phobia, isolation, severe depression where he would sleep all day, not wanting to do anything but talk to me. On my part, there was a lot of reassuring, letting him know everything was going to be okay, and a lot of patience.

It's been almost two years since he went back on medication and life is much more manageable. Panic attacks are very minimal, no more staying in bed; indeed, it's back to work, back to visiting friends and family, back to the man I knew when we first met. As a result of my experience, I have learned that the most important thing you could do for someone with a mental illness is ... TAKE THE TIME AND LISTEN. You will not fully understand what they're going through but just being there and listening to them means the world to them.

A few tips I can offer from my experience:

Do your own research on mental illness, learn all you can, it will help; stay positive, it may be hard at times but it can be done; take care of yourself, you need downtime too because being a carer will wear you out mentally; don't push, recovery needs to happen at their pace not yours; be a good listener – sometimes those with mental illness just need someone to talk to with no advice.

Most importantly of all, never judge. Stigma and prejudice are, without doubt, the biggest enemies of well-being. Love and understanding are everything.

Name: Phil
Age: 35
Location: Aldershot, United Kingdom
Profession: Ambulance Technician, Student Paramedic

I have been involved with pre-hospital emergency care for over 10 years, across various trusts in the UK. In this time I have seen the full spectrum of reactions towards mental health from my colleagues, in both the hospital and pre-hospital environment.

The overriding statement is, 'We are not trained for this.' Still, after all these years, most of my knowledge has come from my own reading and experiences with patients I have met, and hopefully helped. We are trained to recognize conditions and the various sections of the mental health act, but that is usually where it ends. How to interact with patients with mental health conditions, how to spot the 'warning signs' are all skimmed over, we are told that it is something you will pick up on the road, but for that you have to be willing to learn.

Most staff are excellent, and they put 110% into helping the patient, but, as always, there are some that could not care less, or do not understand. I have heard comments like 'Why are we here, it's all in their head?' or 'They are not sick, are they?' I have sent a crewmate back to the vehicle before now because the attitude they projected was making the situation worse, aggravating the patient; that is not what we are there for ...

We need to promote learning, to remove the stigma from mental health that is still prevalent in both the NHS and the population of the UK. I hate to take patients with a mental health crisis to A&E, as it's not the appropriate place for them, and in a way I can understand the look the triage nurse gives me. I know there is little she can do at 3am apart from sit them in a cubicle and keep an eye on them. Mental health patients are becoming more and more common, and quite often at night. Why are the services to help them not 24 hours in most places? We need to be able to help these people whenever and wherever we can, not treat them like an inconvenience and stick them in the corner and forget about them.

And finally, the look of hope on my patients face when I tell them I have been there, I have been in that dark place, and with help and determination I pulled through ...

That is one of the reasons I love my job.

A Day in My Head

Human, All Too Human

There is perhaps one minor consolation for a world of confusion and unpleasantness; *The Truth of Silenus*. Best to have never been born. Or second best, to die early on. Or so Nietzsche explains in *The Birth of Tragedy*. But of course, a world void of hope is not simply unacceptable for those suffering mental ill health alone. The human instinct for self-restoration, to discover life anew; given long enough, there must always be *a will to power*. Our contributors below may not presently see beyond those icy high mountains, formed within the frozen solitude of their lofty minds, but instability has a penchant for oscillation, for reversal. And, of course, we must never forget that without Nietzsche, sceptical as he might have been, there would surely be no Freud ...

Name: Richard
Age: 49
Condition: Obsessive Compulsive Disorder, Depression
Location: York, United Kingdom

Well, I survived another day. It wasn't looking at all hopeful this morning. I woke up with the "staring into the abyss" feeling round about 5.00am (why is it always *then*?). Then I stared at the clock trying to convince myself that the time I had left in bed was about twice as long as it actually was. The minute was on a bad number, as well – one of the death numbers, I think – and the one after that was a bad one too so I had to wait two minutes before I could look at an OK number and neutralise it. At least the death numbers aren't as bad as that *other* number, the one that comes between two bad numbers and isn't itself inherently bad but is terrifying because it just happens to come between the other two. I had to say that number out loud at work the other day and immediately had to whisper a good number to myself to get rid of the tension.

Thank God I don't have a seconds display on my clock – it would be a nightmare. If that really awful number appeared just after I'd woken up, it would screw up the day completely, especially combined with the black dog – OCD complicates depression and vice versa. It's bad enough asking yourself, "Why do I feel like this?", "Am I going to feel like this forever?", without also having to contend with the idea that a random number has derailed your train of thought and ensured that you'll never get an answer to any of those questions.

It's the not knowing that's the worst. Other people don't seem bothered about knowing this stuff but then they're not mentally fighting for their lives every day. I have to know whether me doing things a certain way or thinking a certain way really could set off a chain of events that results in someone else getting ill or dying. I have to know how many germs are on everyday objects and how they can be transferred to other things. Does it just need the slightest contact or something more sustained? How long do germs live on things, anyway? I get through a lot of disinfectant. The palaver of disinfecting bags and suitcases before I go away anywhere is exhausting. Every surface has to be covered inside and out, and still I'm never satisfied that it's safe.

I nearly missed the bus again this morning because I'd been washing my hands so much. I thought I was OK and then put my shoes on at the last minute. Shoes and belts are the dirtiest items of clothing and I hate touching either of them and immediately have to wash or gel my hands. That's another thing – hand hygiene gel. I'm never without it these days but it's a bit of a false friend. I don't like using it in public places either. You do anything with your hands and people's eyes are immediately drawn to it. They don't know I've got OCD but I still feel ashamed – I mean, it's not like I ever see anyone else using the stuff. It makes me feel like a freak.

I'm sure a guy spotted me freezing today as well. I'd been upset by a bad number on a clock which had a second hand. Anyway, I thought I'd got all out of sync so I was waiting for a sound from somewhere to signal that it was safe to carry on. There was just this general background hum for what seemed like ages before I heard a car rev its engine and started walking again. I must look like such an idiot sometimes – freezing, hovering, retracing my steps, going back to objects to tap them a certain number of times, getting "stuck" in doorways. Having said that, it's amazing how many people don't notice. I've told a few friends that I've got OCD and most of them are like "What? Really? I'd never have guessed."

I can't imagine life without OCD now. I can imagine life without depression but it's only very recently that I've felt like that. I carried on for years thinking that depression was just a cross I had to bear until I discovered mindfulness and then changed my medication. I wish it had happened sooner but then I know that some people never really recover from depression and to me that would be like some kind of living hell.

As for OCD it will always be there, I think. It's so powerful, so deeply ingrained. A psychiatrist once told me that it was a very difficult condition to treat. Oh well, let's see what tomorrow brings – a new day to struggle through, I suppose, just as it has for the last 37 years.

A Day in My Head

Name: Tommo
Age: 33
Condition: Obsessive Compulsive Disorder
Location: Suffolk, United Kingdom

I woke up today at about 9am. Today I was going to meet my peer support worker at 2pm to continue sorting through things in my old bedroom at my mum's. My bedroom there needs to be emptied as my mum and stepdad are going to downsize from their current house to a much smaller bungalow.

I have severe OCD and also Asperger's. I've had OCD for about 13 years, since my brother suffered a brain haemorrhage and was left in a persistent vegetative state. I became very worried about making my brother ill, as he was very vulnerable, so I did all that I could to stop myself from passing on germs and making him more unwell.

My OCD has spread and has a very big impact on my life. I used to worry a bit less about making mistakes, but quite soon after leaving university I became terrified of messing up and inadvertently getting into trouble, and have often felt paralysed by fear.

Before moving into supported housing I'd lived at my mum's current home for 14 years. Being a hoarder who loves to collect things and finds it very hard to throw things away, I had ended up with a bedroom there which was still packed full of most of the things I'd collected in the first 30 years of my life. I'd wanted to keep the vast majority of things, but they wouldn't all fit into my flat, unfortunately, which meant I'd have to make some difficult decisions.

Prior to today I'd already sorted through most of the things in my old bedroom, after much help from my peer support worker, support worker, mum and stepdad, but still had an awful lot to do.

Before getting to my mum's today I needed to wash. With my OCD the thing I find hardest is washing myself. I worry about being dirty and contaminating things. At the moment it usually takes about two hours to wash myself, but I usually feel very anxious beforehand and I can often lose hours, and sometimes even days, building up to it. Today is one of those days. I ache a lot through anxiety (as I want to make sure I wash thoroughly enough), so as I often do, I rest on my bed for a while, hoping that I'll feel more relaxed. I'm unable to wash everywhere every day as I would get too sore from washing hard. By the time I've felt able to start washing today I'm already running behind, so arrive at my mum's a lot later than planned.

I get on well with my peer support worker when she arrives, and manage to find quite a lot of paperwork and other things to get rid of. I pack a couple more boxes of things to keep, to take back to my flat. I have a great fear of throwing away things that are important and confidential, so I feel a lot more relaxed if someone I trust checks through things (such as books, magazines and post) with me, as I trust their judgement a lot more than my own.

When I get back to my flat I have to leave my car. I find it a lot harder if I'm going to be leaving it for a long time, as it's more likely that something bad could happen. Before driving I usually have something to eat and drink, and go to the toilet, so that I have a clear head. When I park up, I check the dials on my dashboard are in my preferred positions and that the lights are off and the car is neatly-parked. The things I check the most are that the CD player is turned off, as I worry a lot about getting a flat battery, that the handbrake is on, as I worry a lot about the car running away, and the doors are locked – and, of course, that the windows are shut, so that no one can break in.

Later today I go to the toilet, which is another thing I struggle with as I spend a lot of time checking I'm clean and making sure I've washed my hands thoroughly, as I worry about transferring germs to other things and worry about making me and my family ill. Today this process takes exactly one hour.

I manage to do a load of washing in the evening, which I also find hard. Afterwards I rest on my bed, feeling exhausted, and quickly fall asleep.

Name: Nikki B
Age: 47
Condition: Borderline Personality Disorder
Location: Holts Summit, Missouri, United States

Today woke up with depression kicking in. I climbed out of bed, grabbed some Eggos and chai tea. I ate and went back to bed. My mom calls for me to come over. I'm studying for the peer specialist test, a qualification which will enable me to help others newly diagnosed with a mental illness and/or substance abuse disorder. I already failed once. Not only am I dyslexic and have trouble retaining information, I also take a large dose of Seroquel, which causes me to have memory issues. I haven't showered today but did study with my mom. While at my parents house, I see a person I knew passed away in the paper. She was a local doctor and had brain cancer. I feel jealous she died and not me. I know I should thank my lucky stars I'm alive but depression is such a black hole. I am praying for a manic episode so I clean my house and hopefully get out of bed. But when I return home, I crawl back into bed. Maybe tomorrow I will feel better.

Name: Gemma Sarsfield
Age: 31
Condition: Obsessive Compulsive Disorder, Attention Deficit Hyperactivity Disorder
Location: Manchester, United Kingdom

This is the process of me trying to prepare my meal:

There are a few dirty pots in the sink, clean ones on the drainer and I have pre-prepped my avocado and minced beef; both of these items are in my fridge in tupperware boxes. My intentions right now are to make and eat burritos.

I remove from the fridge my two plastic containers of minced beef and avocado, as well as my salad box. As I take off the lids I cannot be certain that condensation drips didn't fall onto the worktop, so I spray the dishcloth with anti-bacterial spray and wipe down the surface; I then wash my hands. I accidently splash the edge of the sink so I clean it and re-wash my hands. The last bit of mince that I have left looks too greasy so I decide to bin it and I place the empty box in the sink. I fill the sink with hot soapy water and wash the box then re-wash my hands. I spray and wipe the surfaces again. I put my tortillas on a plate then place them in the microwave using only the fingers I haven't touched them with to open and close the door. I then squeeze my hand behind the microwave and strain to switch on the plug with the back of my little finger as it was the only 'clean' part of my hand. I wash my hands whilst they warm up, and I also tackle a few other items in the sink. After one minute the tortillas are warm so I take them out and leave them on the plate. I sprinkle some cheese on the first one, add a handful of salad, then wash my hands so I can open the mackerel packet.

Fish has always played a significant part of my diet but at the same time I really struggle with it because of its oily texture and smell. If I eat it, I always need to brush my teeth or chew gum straight away. I can't touch my mouth or drink from a bottle then touch it again and I will sanitise my mouth and lips after eating fish whenever possible. As I was opening the packet the corner snaps and I am unable to get the mackerel out of the packet easily; I am immediately filled with fear. The only thing I can do is to try and prize it open but in doing so the oil starts to trickle on the work surface and within a few seconds it is also on my hand and has landed on a container.

My frustration and anger shoot up and, as I submerge my hands in the sink, I then have to empty the water out because I am scared that the fish-soaked water will contaminate the cloth and sides of the sink. I simply feel unable to move and my head begins to spin because every move feels terrifying, as if it will have tragic consequences. The only thing I can think to do is cut, so once my hands feel clean, I go into my bathroom and take a knife to my leg and make 4-5 cuts, deep enough to feel satisfied with the pain. I bring myself round by sitting on the floor with my knees to my chest, for almost an hour.

Name: Kaila Ignatius
Age: 23
Condition: Obsessive Compulsive Disorder, Anxiety, Depression
Location: Madison, Wisconsin, United States

So today I Google stalked my abuser for the first time … in ever. She was a teacher when I was in middle school and as soon as I graduated I thought I'd never want to see her face again. In fact, I was actually pretty good at pretending it never even happened.

It was scary typing her name into my phone. As if somehow, like Pandora's box, it was going to open the floodgates to everything shitty in my life again. But when I typed it in nothing happened. I mean, nothing to the supernatural effect. I found her link on a teacher's rating website. Is it bad part of me was hoping to find her name under an obituary post? Not actually wanting her to die. But just knowing that permanently she was somewhere. It still wigs me knowing she's still … *out there* as it were. I'm 23 years old. I have no reason to be afraid. But I am.

I read through her reviews (duh) hoping maybe I'd find someone who had shared my experience. A young pre teen with an energetic personality and love for the limelight, finding themselves suddenly victimized; someone who left school most days crying; someone who faked-sick just to get out of class; someone else with thousands of dollars worth of therapy and pills that only helps them cope but never to truly move past what happened; someone else who sees that angry, scrunched up face spitting insults at them but can't hear the words because they blocked them out to keep their own sanity; someone else who was isolated and publicly humiliated in front of all their peers; someone who was taught that what made them different was a poison that was killing their chances of ever surviving in this world.

A Day in My Head

I want to know if they shut down or if they kept fighting back like me. I want to know if they had any friends to help them through. I want to know what kind of mental health problems they have. Did you get OCD? Depression? Anxiety? Did you try to kill yourself? How long after the abuse started did you wait for your first attempt? Did you cut yourself? Did you dig your nails in your skin? Did you wear a sweater and high knee socks with your uniform to cover them up? Did you find yourself years later in a high school bathroom trying to choke yourself because you just wanted to pass out and get away from everything? I want to know if they ever hurt anyone, and if they ever tried to reach out to their victims. I want to know if the cycle of abuse stopped with them. I want to know if they sung songs in their head to drown out the hate. I want to know if they practiced insults they'd sling back. I want to know if they ever used them. I want to know if they ever drew horrible pictures of her being tortured that the other teachers found and did nothing about. I want to know if they imagined her dying. I want to know if they fantasize about it today. I want to know if they think just as much as I do about what I would say to a crowd full of people there to mourn her death. Would they spit on the remains of her intact image? Would they act like St. Maria and lay a lily for stab wound?

When I go on I'm disappointed to find only three reviews. Two positive, one negative, all focused on her teaching abilities. I found myself doubting myself again. I must have made it all up. I'm exaggerating. I'm a drama queen. If there's no one to corroborate my feelings then they never were there in the first place ...

They only knew her as a teacher. I knew her as a machine. I knew her as a cold woman. And now I know her the way only one broken soul can reach out to another. It got me thinking that maybe abusers are just looking for someone to drag into hell with them. As an abuser, you don't see them as a victim, you see them as a comfort object. Like a blanket to hold when you're scared, they become a safety net. I'm no longer suffering alone. I have another broken soul with me.

It's been 10 years and I'm still broken. I'm cracked in so many places and I worry if I'll ever be whole again or if I'll just have to find a way to become stronger at the broken places.

Name: Jade Goddard
Age: 17
Condition: Borderline Personality Disorder
Location: Birmingham, United Kingdom.

Yesterday I found myself lying in a deep bath with a razor blade to my wrists, ready to slice *down* and not across this time, but instead I took it out on my legs.

A short while back, I contemplated overdosing for ages until one day, of course, I actually impulsively did it just to prove a point, grabbing the first pills I saw and just necking back as much as I could. That was until these *hands* grabbed and restrained me; lucky for them it was only Mebeverine, not so lucky for me. They still mock me, the voices inside. "You can't even kill yourself properly … even when you take an overdose it's still just as much of a joke as your life is … you NEED to get hold of some of those anti depressants, they will do the job properly."

So the only thing I can do to stop them is to inflict constant pain on myself, but, hey, at least my legs have cool scars, at least others will know I'm an attention seeker. The constant battle between distinguishing what the voices think and what I think is taking its toll on me, maybe I should just end it, I won't have to listen to their shit anymore, I'm just so tired.

Name: Veronica Gavan
Age: 22
Condition: Manic Depressive Disorder, General Anxiety
Location: Lompoc, California, United States

Dear Diary,

Today, I feel ... blank. I have a million exciting things going on in my life but I feel nothing toward them. No excitement, no anger, no happiness, just a deep emptiness. The past few nights have been rough. It's a constant and incongruous battle of knowing, on the one hand, I am strong enough to fight the self doubt and yet, on the other, dealing somehow with the thoughts relating to a lack of self worth. At least college is over. No more days of being too depressed to get up, yet being all too anxious about not doing well enough in my classes. My thoughts and feelings can be so conflicting ...

In seven days, I will be getting married. I should be happy ... I know this is the best thing that has happened since the hospitalization but I can't be. I feel a lingering exhaustion, I've been sleeping too much to pass the days when I feel like there's nothing inside.Being numb is better than fighting the anxiety. No panic attacks lately, but they are always looming. It starts with a feeling of dread, allowing the

A Day in My Head

physical reactions and thoughts to take over. This delays any sense of reality.

This is a short entry, but that's all I have. It's hard to explain the emotions inside when today they were nothing.

Name: 'Timothy Rosen'
Age: 30
Condition: General Anxiety, Body Dysmorphic Disorder
Location: Canvey Island, United Kingdom

Follicular Atrocities; A postmodern nightmare

I awake this morning in my single bed (with its own comfortable pull-out trundle for guests) in full remembrance of a dream I'd had only moments earlier. This is highly unusual, I think to myself, as I triumphantly review like a friendly Stanley Kaufmann, my slumber-induced Blockbuster, because usually you forget dreams instantly; like grains of sand through the lithesome fingers of a child – especially the ones involving anthropomorphic sex with cats. But today, well today is different.... [Note to reader: I have opted in true postmodern style to write this entry as a stream-of-consciousness, which means the preceding long-winded and clumsy introduction is *perfectly* permissible).

Anyway, back to this morning. The dream. In this extremely well directed dream, generated by a clearly very gifted brain, I was sitting in a hairdressers salon in America and had simply asked for something a tad more stylish – I can offer no more detail than that – which, as luck would have it, was enough to prompt the attractive woman about to cut my hair, and now looking at me with a rather dangerous glint in her dark brown smokey eye – as if up to something dastardly – to say, "OK."

[Note to reader: I have never understood how one's own somnolent brain can direct a movie inside one's own head, carefully craft the dialogue, etc., etc., whilst you, always the protagonist or some Avatar-esque other (often of the same sex, though I do once remember being a woman and having tits, which made me want to flagellate aggressively) remain utterly clueless as to what is coming next. If that isn't proof that Descartes wasn't talking hairy balls, I don't know what is ...]

ANYWAY ... Back to the hairdressers, and the smiley *coiffeuse*, who had an air of confidence about her, picked up a pair of stainless steel sharp-tipped scissors and started going gently but firmly at my hair. Snip snip snip, went the scissors. She must've cut three strands of hair. Then, just as she was about to snip again for a fourth time, she said, "Actually, it's a bit grubby, your hair. Stinks of shit. We probably need to wash it first." And before I had the chance to do or say anything at all, she had thrown a large washing up bowl full of tepid water over my head whilst simultaneously injecting me in the arm with an unknown substance. I passed out like Michael Jackson in concert ...

When I awoke, everything had changed. My appearance was totally different. Instead of a mop of unruly curly hair, there was a top knot. Instead of a curly, variegated beard, there was a dark brown manicured scruff. And on both arms, instead of (curly) arm hairs, there were tattoo sleeves.

I looked uncannily like one of those indie kids who wears too much flannel plaid and eats artisanal seafood from *Ortiz* jars.

Immediately, I began panicking and convulsing on the floor until … I awake in a cold sweat. It is over. No top knot. No tattoos. I am still my curly, unattractive self ...

*

First Snip (Is the deepest)

The last body modification involving a sharp instrument and also done *ex parte* (at least in spirit) was my *briss* - or circumcision to the uninitiated. I remember the incident well ...

My mum was actually a tad worried because the midwife had already diagnosed me with 'a bit of a sniffle'. So just before the circumcision was due to commence, frightened of the consequences of my being poorly whilst under the knife, my mum consulted with Dr Gull, our family GP, to check whether it would still be prudent to go ahead. Fortunately, it didn't take much for Dr Gull to reassure her that removing a perfectly operative element of my genitalia would be just fine, regardless of my sniffle: "If he does have a cold," he tells her with aplomb, "then he'll have a cold *and* a sore willy."

The cause of my anxiety perhaps? It seems fanciful. After all, I have maintained a fully monogamous relationship with the soft porn on female flatulence sites for many a happy year. Not to mention the fact that my best friend, Yacob, had to remove *his* foreskin in later life, due to it being tight, which was far, far worse. Nevertheless, it must be said, my relationship with religion has been dicey ever since. Like so many good Jews, I am an atheist now. But it was not always so ...

A Day in My Head

I remember being 12 years old (a year before my Bar mitzvah, in which my family celebrated me singing Hebrew up on the *Bima* and gave me a not-too-shabby start to my bank balance). We were in Jewish Sunday school, known as Chedar (spelt almost like the cheese but pronounced as if drowning in catarrh), where the Rabbi happened to be doing a demonstration for *Sukkot*, with a *Lulav* in one hand and an *Etrog* in the other. Behind me, one of the naughty kids, who also happened to be my second cousin, was playing up something rotten on account of him being a 'lobus'. This was, invariably, how his parents would refer to him. A *'Shhh ... shhh ... schnitzel',* was the Rabbi's own designation. I was *certain* he deserved what came next ...

In my best Tony Montana impersonation, I wrestled this 5ft *schnitzel* to the ground in what can only be described as a gloriously orchestrated headlock (which I'd learned play fighting my dad in the garden), and immediately witnessing this sudden outbreak of *chamas* before his very eyes, the Rabbi wrapped up the recitation, waved vigorously the Lulav and Etrog in accordance with the blessing, placed said Lulav and Etrog carefully and delicately onto the table before him (in the case of the etrog, stem down, pitam up), finished another blessing apropos the hide of Leviathan or some such, recited *Amen* a few more times, bowed his head, straightened his *kippah* and then rushed over as quickly as he possibly could to the source of the commotion ...

The two of us were immediately pulled apart.

When I got home that afternoon, at the behest of both my concerned parents, I phoned the Rabbi to plead for forgiveness. And, to my surprise, the bearded Anglo-Jew from St Annes who always began each sentence with *Baruch Hashem* was faultlessly acquitting. "If I'm honest," he said, sounding nothing if not a tad worn, "the little ... shhh ... shhh ... *schnitzel* deserved it."

It was enough there and then to galvanise my conviction. We were an eye for an eye people. We were The Hebrews. With curly hair, strange nostrility* and plenty of *chazaq*.

(*I myself have an aquiline nose. The first girl I loved had a retrousse nose. It was never going to work.)

Humpty-Dumpty

Despite being at times pugnacious, I was as delicate as beech tree bloom in Spring when it came to issues of self-esteem. Or, more aptly, my appearance. During High School - an all boy's grammar in Essex where they subdivided you into arcane 'Houses' – I was teased about the shape of my head on a regular basis which was, so they said, the shape of a hardboiled egg. One morning during Religious Education, I remember one of the popular boys in my class, with dents in each cheek (passing for dimples), told me he was going to inflict maximum damage onto my unseemly, overweight ('puppy fat') carcass. The remark came almost out of the blue, sometime after I had finished carefully explaining to the class *The Seven Laws of Noah* for Key Stage 2: *Judaism*. "You're Dead, Egg Head," he told me, with palpable menace. His evil white irises shimmered like egg whites across a sea of desks. I was making up egg comparisons in my head already.

Of course, being a descendant of the 2nd Century Maqabim, *A Hebrew*, I was quite happy to fight the boy with dented cheeks and egg white irises on the school playground – until at least one of us had a bloody nose and had to go in. Though it never really came to it. Fighting in a grammar school, at any rate, was prohibited. Alongside yo-yos, Pokémon cards and menstrual cycles – the female teachers were also men. Nevertheless, the damage - *emotional* damage that is - had already been done. From that day on I felt truly *ugly*. My nickname *egghead* had unfortunately stuck like yoke to bread soldiers. And, as with all cases of childhood bullying, so too would the feelings of low self-esteem.

Interpreter of Dreams

Awaking from my dream, I remain in bed for a further few minutes. A thought attends. If I were truly free to do whatever the hell I liked, I'd go on Saccharine binges and sleep with whores. Would a good dose of gorging and humping and licking and fucking make all the difference? Change me somehow. I feel like I want to 'test' the theory out but I won't. The anxiety would be too much.

Later today, I attend counselling. I decide I will tell my therapist about my dream. She seats me down by a rickety table with a bottle of pretend Évian-les-Bains, filled instead with ozonated tap water, and asks me how I have been. Afterwards, she proffers her opinion pertaining to my night-time exploits.

"I think your subconscious is trying to tell you something … I think it is telling you that you frantically yearn to change and yet lack distinctly the courage to do so. That you are journeying around and around in ever diminishing concentric circles and eventually you may well just disappear up into your own …"

I remind her politely that she is a CBT therapist and should probably leave the clairsentience to the woman who does Wheel of Destiny for *The Sun* …

A Day in My Head

If this were *The Glass Bead Game*, a book written by an agreeable German *anti-Nazi*, I might genuinely be considered a master player. A distinguished member of an austere Order of pure intellectuals. But in the *real* world, outside of any intellectual ivory towers, in a world of urban decay and dating sites for vegetarians, things are so much harder. In this world, my face and body are every bit as important as my brain, if not more so. And especially, of course, when it comes to getting laid …

I walk past Boots on the way home and decide to invest in the smallest pot of 'beard oil' made of jojoba and coconuts for a tenner before off to a popular High-street name to buy some conducive items of clothing and to look at myself from the side in the changing room mirrors. My aquiline nose looks even more aquiline from the side, which depresses me further. Back-to-back, my dad reckons my brother and I resemble a pick-axe. Life is shit. I gaze at my reflection, exaggerated by the terrible lighting. *Oy Gevalt*, I look like a boiled egg who has told too many porkie pies (both lying and the touching of pig carcasses being strictly forbidden, of course - see *Leviticus*). Though the only person I have perhaps truly ever lied to is myself. It is probably about time I faced up to the uncomfortable truth, a truth which for over a decade I have wished and lamented and begged and wished, like Harry Block (Woody Allen), lamenting his newly 'out-of-focus' form in *Deconstructing Harry*, (see *Leviticus*) was merely a figment of my own neurotic imagination:

That I, Timothy Frank *Sh'mu'el* Rosen, am probably – almost certainly – going to fail the very essential tenets of *natural selection*.

Name: Alice Robinson
Age: 25
Condition: Obsessive Compulsive Disorder
Location: Sheffield, United Kingdom

It's the start of another exhausting week, in which I act like there is nothing but happiness, kittens and rainbows navigating their way through my thoughts. Today was tough; working in mental health and having my own problems is getting more difficult. It's just getting too hard to lie. Everyone knows I'm an anxious person but I don't think they understand the extent of it.

Anyway, today started like any other; I woke up, partly disappointed that I actually woke up again, and got in the shower with a heavy heart. As I washed, the images started. Graphic images in which I slip in the bath and smash my head on the side of it, blood rushing out of my head as I lie unconscious. I closed my eyes, blurred the image, blinked and shook my head, trying to make it go away. It wouldn't go, it replayed and replayed. My number, 27: 2+7=9, [9x2=18, 1+8=9], [9x7=63, 6+3=9] so 9+9+9=27. Then I could carefully get out of the shower and dress in the 'right' order to make sure nothing bad would happen today.

I said goodbye to Tom but I couldn't tell him I love him because that would mean that I would never see him again. *If I say it, he will die on the way to work. But if I don't say it then he will think I don't love him.* Such an agonising impasse. And so I left without saying it. I'd rather he was alive. *Does that mean I don't love him? Should we be together? What if he's cheating on me? Does he even love me? When did he last say it?*

I drove to work, dreading the day, wondering why I'm in a job that causes me so much stress and is so overwhelming. I pulled up, took a deep breath and walked in, plastering a fake smile on my face, hoping that no-one could see through it. Only eight and a half hours till the end of the act.

Somehow, I got through the day, graphic images pouring through my head as I talked to my patients with their own mental health problems. *I looked down at her breasts. Does that mean I'm attracted to her? Am I a lesbian? I'm sure I'm not, I'm sure I like men but I don't know now.* I doubt everything I think. I don't know what's true anymore and it's scary. I battled through my work and called my patients from last week to tell them what treatment they'd be getting. But I couldn't dial. *No, I made a mistake, type it again. That didn't feel right, start again. Did I press nine or did I press something else? The screen says nine but I should start again just to make sure. I thought about the number seven when I meant to press three so I must have typed it wrong.*

I feel like I'm losing my grip and my brain is telling me I'm a bad person. Every bad thought I have is evidence that I'm a bad person. And if I write certain thoughts down, they will come true, harm will come to my loved ones and it will be my fault, so I have to stop that happening in any way I can. I'm constantly thinking about how I am responsible for the well-being of the people I love. *I must check she is OK or something will have happened to her. I need to get dressed in the right order or he will die. I need to message him or he will kill himself. If I pick up a knife I will lose control and stab him. Did I put poison in his drink while I was making it? If I have these thoughts, does it mean I want to hurt people? I must be a bad person and I need to die. I am evil. If I don't kill myself I will end up hurting someone. It's for the safety of everyone else.*

Sometimes the thoughts get too much and I think about ending my life. Sometimes it would just be easier. Sometimes it feels like the only option. I don't know what has stopped me so far, and part of me wishes I had the courage to do it. But most of me wishes I had the courage to carry on and the courage to get through this, regain my ambition and help others get through their difficulties. Right now I just need to get through tomorrow.

Name: Willow Knight
Age: 25
Condition: Bipolar Disorder II
Location: London, United Kingdom

It is 11:59pm on May 16, 2016, and I'm sitting on my bed, surrounded by multiple packs of pills, listening to my 20-year old sister stumbling around, having returned home from a drunken event after work. If I ever needed a sign that my life has taken a twisted turn thanks to my mental illness, it's presently gulping down water one door down. She attends the university I had to withdraw from, she's currently working in a job that I once would have held (with a close family friend), and, as proven by tonight, she's able to enjoy a drink whenever she likes. Instead of holding down a job and working on a university degree, I have had to return to England and live with my parents, spend a month in a hospital, and attend weekly therapy sessions until the end of time.

Today was a strange day. My sleep has been ruined lately, probably due to heightened anxieties with an extra person in the house (said drunk sister), and so I fell asleep very late last night. I have also found myself falling into an old habit – binge watching episodes of whatever television show I've found holds my attention. At the moment it is, embarrassingly, *Made in Chelsea*. The chosen show means that I don't have to think about my own problems, and it keeps me busy and away from negative and destructive urges.

It's here that I'd go on to explain exactly what happened today, and exactly how difficult I found the day, even though I did almost nothing, and how I'd go into detail about my recent hospitalisations (four in the past 12 months), but I can't really. As I've learned in therapy recently (thanks!) I have a "be perfect" driver that is behind every single thing that I do. Even though there is no pressure on this short piece of writing, I feel it HAS to be perfect. It has to be witty, it has to get my point across, it has to be the perfect number of words – and those, by the way, have to be an odd number, thanks to the OCD from which I suffer – and it has to make you understand my illness. But I am actually learning from this therapy that I am undergoing. I have decided that it's more important to get this down on paper (electronic, that is) than for it to be… perfect. So I'll try to finish this, and I'll be quick, but I won't like it.

I don't like change. I've moved a lot in the past eight years, and it has affected me more than I have realised. Packing is a huge trigger for me, and it basically makes me shut my mind down (unhelpful). However, it has also shown me that I am semi-useless when plans change. Today, four things changed in my schedule, one of which was a "throw your clothes on you're supposed to be getting your blood taken *right now*" appointment, and by the end of the day, I was drained. My brain can't deal with the switching from one persona to another; the girl that lies in bed, half asleep, watching *Made in Chelsea*, and the girl who is relatively normal, who can interact with the phlebotomist as if she isn't taking her blood to test her Lithium levels. I am constantly switching to a different facet of my personality depending on the situation, and it is just exhausting. Bipolar disorder affects everyone differently, but for me, I am constantly in a state of flux. I suffer from (depending on who you ask) either bipolar II, or bipolar spectrum disorder. Both mean that I don't have extended episodes of mania, but short bursts. I do, however, have extended episodes of depression – that can land me in the hospital.

May 16th was, really, an ordinary day. I had previously been in therapy on Mondays but cancelled that after I realised it was doing more harm than good (it's very far away, and the groups were not helping), so I was simply at home with my dad. However, writing about it, and realising the things that affected me, and pushing through to finish this, makes a huge difference. Readers might not learn much from my experience but I did and, at the moment, that's what matters.

Name: Stephen Bowles
Age: 62
Condition: Obsessive Compulsive Disorder
Location: West Yorkshire, United Kingdom
My days are always predictable. I always have to face the challenge of coping with OCD. This horrendous illness has been with me now for more than 50 years. I have lost count of the number of times that I have thought to myself that I cannot take any more. I do, however, keep going, taking the punishment, living with the brain torture that never ends.

The day begins with a bathroom routine that only occasionally takes me less than two hours. My own personal hygiene, cleaning the toilet and the bath, takes me such a long time. I feel I am rushing but it takes so long. I am exhausted by the time I finish.

The next task is preparing my dinner. I hate peeling the vegetables. A slight splash of water on my hair would necessitate washing my hair. If the water were to hit my clothes I would want to change them. I hate doing any cleaning jobs in the house as I do not want to touch so many things. My brain is in turmoil as I try to avoid touching items in my house. I take the rubbish out to the wheelie-bin, dreading a fly will land

A Day in My Head

on me. After that most unpleasant of jobs I wash my hands, arms and face in order to feel comfortable.

What I have described above is the relatively easy aspect of coping with my OCD. Dirt and contamination are bad enough, but the brain torture, for me, is even worse. Words or images can trigger a feeling of being unclean. I then have to wash. Within seconds, while still wet, the thought or image may return so I have to wash again. I may repeat the washing ritual until I feel exhausted. I spend the day hoping the thoughts will not "get through" and that I will be able to avoid the "decontamination." Occasionally, I go a day without giving in to the need to wash. Usually, I give in many times as the feeling of being dirty is just too much to tolerate.

My day might include shopping. Standing in queues is unpleasant. People might come too close. Very often people cough without covering their mouths or come very close wearing filthy trainers. Flailing walking-sticks and pram wheels are enough to cause me to flee and lose my place in the queue. The worse scenario for me is the need to use public toilets. I always say that the British are a nation of toilet foulers. I rarely find a toilet that is acceptable, so end up returning home to have a bath and a change of clothes.

Going to a restaurant is something I like to do. What I do not like is seeing children climbing on the seats wearing shoes that have walked the filthy streets. One restaurant I used to go to had a drawer where people collected their knives and forks. One day I saw a man leave the toilet cubicle, not wash his hands and then put his hands into the drawer to get his knife and fork. I asked a member of staff to wash my knife and fork after explaining what I had seen. I stopped going to the restaurant because I no longer felt comfortable there.

We are told exercise is good for us. The problem for me is that most public footpaths are not clean. I have to watch very carefully where I am walking. Windy days are even worse because I am dreading any of the litter blowing onto me. If that happened, a bath and change of clothes would be needed. The contaminated clothes would have to be washed thoroughly in a bowl filled with disinfectant, even before been put into the washing machine. For the reasons I have given I avoid going out. I cannot remember the last time I visited a park or walked on grass. What I do remember very well is an occasion when I was walking through Leeds and a plastic bag was blowing along the pavement towards me. As it got near I jumped up to let the bag pass under my feet. The people who were at the bus stop nearby started laughing!

I have to cope with my OCD as best I can. I cannot beat it so I just accept it. I wish my life had been different. I have had so many years of unhappiness. There have been so many lost opportunities.

Name: Ellie Lloyd Jones
Age: 26
Condition: Borderline Personality Disorder, Anorexia, Depression and Anxiety
Location: Salisbury, United Kingdom
Profession: University Graduate – Unemployed

The moment when you begin to wake up, drifting between the nightmares that forbid any rest and your exhausted reality; fading in and out of consciousness, slowly coming round to face the fact that your reality is, in fact, a nightmare from which you cannot escape. You have to rise to fight once again, knowing full well that your internal bully is about to wake too. I wake up, once again, wishing that I hadn't.

Basic functioning like dressing, showering, and eating, feel like insurmountable challenges, so you commit minimal effort to other necessary tasks just so as to appear like a functioning adult and without using up all of your limited energy resources. After several attempts, from the outside I look "normal".

The voice of disorders plays havoc with your mind, trying their hardest to sabotage your day and your prolonged attempt at recovery. Hurling insults at every move you make, you can't seem to get anything right. You tell yourself that these are just thoughts, that they are not real, but they infiltrate your belief system and you can no longer tell what is real and what is not.

Plans for the day hold dread and anxiety, but without them you face a day of isolation, with only your thoughts as company. You don't want to spend time with anyone, but the person you least want to spend time with is yourself. It's almost better to pretend to be alright, to put on "the front" for others, than to be alone not being alright. But the vast level of energy expenditure needed to sustain "the front", leaves you exhausted and vulnerable to default back to destructive coping strategies. Today I choose to act, today I have to be "OK".

The drive to meet a friend from the past saps energy through forced concentration. The bubbling anxiety poisoning my thoughts and blood stream with adrenaline and cortisol, self-doubt spreading like wildfire. You beam a smile and hope that it's more convincing than it feels, making laughable attempts at small talk. When asked how things have been, you

A Day in My Head

long to explain things have been better but life's looking up! But the broken record of mental ill-health repeats its tired song: I'm no further forward than I was when we last met three years back. I'm tired beyond exhaustion, I can't sleep, I can't eat, I can't feel anything positive, I'm drowning in a sea of self-hatred, I'm not sure this life is for me. Somehow, a shrug, saying "things are OK, I guess ... gotta keep keeping on," and a change of subject seem to be the best option, followed by a fond goodbye and a quick exit.

Back at home, back with the raging rampage of thoughts that blind you, back with the bully that won't stop criticizing your performance, you lie victim to your mind. Eventually, the only safe option is to go to sleep, even though it's only mid-afternoon. You try to justify it by convincing yourself that you are tired and a sleep will help. Let's face it, fewer hours in the day that you have to fight can only be a good thing, and skipping lunch always makes you feel better.

After a few uncomfortable hours, a run seems like a good idea. It might soothe some of the torturous disordered thoughts, offer a subtle form of self-harm, pleasing the need for self-punishment without active destruction, work off some of the adrenaline from earlier and release some endorphins to combat the darkness. But remember: you did 10k last time, so best hit 11k this time.

The evening's demons take on the scariest form. With the evening hours lasting much longer than the day's, your fight has to up its game. At last, you reach a time that would be seen as an acceptable bedtime, and then the hours seem to fly by taking you into the small hours. You hit overtired and then trying to get sleep becomes impossible, with your mind racing off into the future and back into the past. Guided into sleep by medication, my mind finally falls quiet.

I am free until the morning.

Name: Justine McNeil
Age: 23
Condition: Depression, Social Anxiety and Generalized Anxiety Disorder
Location: Ontario, Canada

It's 6:00am, my alarm is going off and the feeling of dread has already hit me. For a while I actually thought this had started to relent, this waking up nauseous just thinking about having to go to work and not knowing what the day might hold, but here I am lacking even the energy to pull myself out of bed and wanting to cry at the thought of facing the day. It's so hard to get up, go to work each morning and pretend that everything is okay when the truth is, since the beginning of April, I have been stuck in one of the worst bouts of depression I have had in a long time. In the back of my mind I am constantly worrying about my upcoming trip to India, thinking of every possible worst case scenario, getting headaches when I think about having to meet a group of strangers, let alone live with them for three weeks. "What are they going to think of me?", "Will I fit in?", "Will they be too loud or too big a group for me to handle?" My joints are physically aching because I have been bottling this up for so long.

Monday at work always feels like the longest day and today it seems like I can't do anything right. Within the first hour I am in the back room almost in tears because it is all just too overwhelming. Noises seem to be amplified today, every little thing is making me agitated, and while I know I shouldn't take it personally, I almost want to run out of the room when the secretary is short with me. It's days like today that make me want to just quit and go home, but I know I need to earn money. I stay up night after night worrying about how I am going to pay for things, how I am ever going to afford to move out or get a new car and about how burdensome I am to my family. By the time my break rolls around I am absolutely exhausted and just want to crawl into bed. When I call my mom just to say "hi" I can tell by her tone of voice that she isn't having a good day either. I apologise like I always do in such situations and then want to scream when she says it's silly, and not to mention weird, that I am apologising. As much as she says she understands the depression I live with, it is comments such as this that make me realise she doesn't. There are so many things that I can't help doing, such as constantly apologising for everything that happens, constantly feeling guilty and always being on edge.

By the time I head back to work my head is absolutely pounding and all my medication seems to be doing today is just making me feel sick. I am exhausted from a lack of sleep and already irritated, so this, combined with a loud room full of kids, puts me completely on edge. I feel bad about being so strict with them sometimes, but I constantly worry that something bad is going to happen to someone I know, which is the original cause of my anxiety, and I just want to keep them all safe and to please everybody. By the time I get home I feel like a zombie, all my emotions are drained, I feel purposeless and so it's another day without blogging or tweeting. It makes me question why I even bother being an advocate when I don't seem to be making a difference. When I feel like this I am always brought back to the time when I was laughed at for telling someone my dream. It just seems like a vicious, hopeless cycle that isn't getting any better, and as I fall asleep with tears in my eyes I can only dream that tomorrow might be better.

Name: Ilona
Age: 19
Condition: Borderline Personality Disorder

I woke up and it was 2am. It was semi-dark and the first thing I remember is that I felt so panicked even reaching the light switch next to my bed felt like running a marathon. I left the light on to fall asleep again. Next time I awoke it was actually morning. Checking my phone and seeing a message from my mum. Hating myself and her, for making me hate myself, simultaneously. Doing something, anything, to distract myself, maybe reading a book, going for a walk, doing some art, watching TV, trying to block out the bad feelings, reality. Not successful, obviously. It's midday and I'm already tired.

Looked at the works of people who are more successful than me online. Very inspiring and finally got me feeling sad about something different. Found an actual reason to hate myself. Feels oddly good. For a moment or two.

I'm so alone. I wish someone would come and hold me, be there with me, just be there. I feel so abandoned. But I can't ask anyone. I don't have any right to. It won't do any good. Besides, they all leave sometime. Always, they always leave sometime. Maybe after months, weeks. Perhaps after only days, hours. But they leave. I can't ask anyone to come, I'm too afraid that they'll leave. And I know they will, I understand that they have to, in the logical part of my mind. The part of me that feels abandoned, however, doesn't register the logic. That part will pretty much always feel abandoned, no matter what you (have to) do.

I feel bad. I am crying on the bathroom floor. It's too late to call anyone. I can't. I want to cut. But if I cut I won't find the strength to do something bigger, something better. If I cut I'll live. I want to cut, but I want to cut enough, for ... forever. And I know I can't.

I see someone in the mirror and I wonder why I look so ridiculous. Seeing this figure, just looking so outwardly sad makes me feel nothing but disgust for the one in the mirror, for me.

I want security. I am desperate for someone to help me be safe. I can't provide myself the safety I need. I try to, try *hard*. I can't ask anyone for help though. If I *ask* then I will be provided with the additional security I so desperately crave, which is perhaps all too easy and would instantly render me undeserving.

The next day I wake up and yesterday's sorrow and despair just seems like a bad dream, something unreal. I can't believe the part of myself that is still so exhausted and scared. It wasn't *that* bad. It can't have been that bad or how come I'm still here. You must have made it up, you pathetic little shit. But part of me knows that's not true. And so I fight for recognition within myself.

And outside too. Because, really, I can't be that bad can I? Still integrated in society, doing a job, no criminal record. Hobbies, friends and "all the fun stuff you say you enjoy". I do. I love my job. Love my hobbies. Am passionate about stuff, interested in politics. But I suffer. Some days more than others. No matter how great the holiday is, no matter how much I enjoy it, my demons will have travelled with me. But just because they do it doesn't mean I won't take something positive from that holiday. Truth is a complex thing.

There are reasons I do some things differently from others. I try not to overload you, my friend or family member, but maybe I should. Maybe you could then, finally, see the overload I'm dealing with every day. Maybe you could stop making what I do to help myself about you. It's not. It's not you. It's me and my life.

Name: Sanchita Islam/Q S Lam

Age: 43
Condition: Schizoaffective Disorder
Location: London, Brussels, Kuala Lumpur
Profession: Artist, Published Writer, Commissioned Filmmaker, Director of International Arts Organisation pigmentexplosion, Mental Health Campaigner and Author of *Schizophrenics Can Be Good Mothers Too* (Muswell Hill Press, 2015)

Woke up around 3.30am, but then I did go to bed at 8.30pm. Since March 17th my sleeping has veered dangerously off track; last night was the first time in weeks that I managed to sleep at a reasonable time and not wake up after a couple of hours. This is progress in my eyes since sleep impacts profoundly on my state of mind.

Strange dreams perturb and I cringe when I think of my manic garrulousness of the previous evening.

A Day in My Head

It is still night, although early morning, I am at my desk poised to paint; even though I have a more pressing deadline pending.

Each day I am tormented by the list of things that Fred, the voice in my head, taunts me todo. His demands are incessant and I usually obey. It wouldn't hurt to go back to sleep and wake at 6am but no, I have to paint.

Welcome to my world, where words and art pour for no apparent reason. As I work, Fred tells me to do other things; he continues to harangue me with endless tasks that are impossible to fulfil in a lifetime, even if you worked every second of the day until the minute you drop dead. Most days I am debilitated and paralysed by the prospect of fulfilling Fred's demands.

Some say Fred is an arsehole. I wonder if Fred would be happy if I did jump from the top of my building; he tells me to kill myself almost daily, but here I am, still very much alive

The biggest consequence of dealing with my mental health problems is this sense of being inherently different from other people. Simple tasks that we take for granted, like saying hello, can elude me in specific circumstances. I can go years without talking to family members. Privately, you think you are protecting them from Fred, yet you pine for contact and understanding. The solitude of these hours is comforting - temporarily liberated by the social expectations involuntarily thrust upon me.

The demands of day-to-day living evaporate when I'm alone with the canvas and a curious, protracted dialogue ensues, resulting in an image that begins to be born. My creations become something real and tangible that I can see, instead of the internal mental nonsense that ties me in knots.

When I was younger I used to sing with my sisters; we would perform - I had no fear. Then at age 11, a stranger told me I was rubbish so I stopped singing overnight. Since the psychosis of 2009, I started singing again. Sometimes I just make up compositions; I am not sure what to call them - wailings... cries from the gut. After my two-year-old son went to crèche, I lay on my bed and began to sing, recording whatever came out of my mouth.

Now daylight has cut through the darkness, the birds are tweeting, there's an interminable din in my head, an overwhelming sense that however hard I try, I will always fail. The light is blinding. Daytime is discombobulating; already I long for the comfort of night. Although awake, my eyes are swollen and sore from fatigue - sometimes I wish I could sleep forever.

But going back to sleep - even though I want the insults to stop, the demands to stop, everything to stop - is not an option. Must stay awake and trudge through the day. This work that I do and these deadlines that I scramble to meet must presumably mean something to someone. That's what I tell myself. Stay alive to raise your children, to make art, to write, even if you are residing in a mental daily hell. And it's a hell that's almost impossible to describe.

The day is like a blur until the children return; I pick up my son from crèche, then we cycle down the hill to pick up my eldest child (he's at Lego club). Then I try to do what normal mothers might do and take them for sushi, observing their bickering while struggling to maintain my cool. When we reach home, after dodging the rain, we all sit together studying Bangla, as my little one scribbles with coloured pens. We read and go on an impromptu excursion before they go to bed at 7.30pm. My husband appears and disappears; I retreat to my studio exhausted, knowing that I will wake again in the early hours and drift to my desk
to tackle the painting that stares at me stubbornly, demanding to be finished - and still the whir in my head persists, it never ceases.

No Matter What

There are those in our lives who give us strength, who provide warmth and companionship during times of near-Hyperborean isolation. And for no group is this more important, so desperately needed, than those experiencing symptoms of mental ill health ... "A friend is one who walks in when others walk out," says Walter Winchell. Our family and friends are perhaps the greatest antidote to the pain of loneliness.

Name: Tim Jenkins
Age: 54
Condition: Daughter's Obsessive Compulsive Disorder, Misophonia
Location: Manchester, United Kingdom

The first question of the day is how she will be feeling in herself today – my beautiful 16 year old girl, who's approaching her GCSE exams. She's blonde and pretty and clever but not so pretty when she snarls and sneers and spits out insults and invective. Not so clever when she's irrational and utterly self-obsessed. Her presence in the house dominates everything. Her mood each day impacts on everything.

Sometimes she is quite sunny and co-operative; other days she's stressed and her illness is manifest from the first unreasonable shout through a bedroom door. 'Are you up and awake, gorgeous?' Oh dear, damn ... going to be one of those days, is it?

The second question: how am I? I don't always sleep well. I don't always retire sober, so often I'm a bit tired and 'heady'. I have a living to make, I have two other teenage children to parent, and a dog to walk – we got her to help with the illness. It worked really well in the short term actually; a massive incentive to motivate her to really difficult achievements - but not anymore. And yet the dog still needs walking!

My partner always does retire sober because her drinking got so out of hand, a spectacular meltdown, when the pressure finally boiled over, meaning she *had* to quit. She simply can't risk saying again the things she screamed and sobbed at our daughter about how hard it is to live with her. She didn't really mean them, of course - she'd sacrifice herself in a heartbeat for her - but life would be so much easier if she *hadn't* ever been born.

Actually, of course, she has sacrificed herself for her daughter - the jobs she wasn't able to take. And the holiday's we haven't been able to take or were utterly ruined. How many times can you insist on trying for a family day out before you give up? How many times do you say "we'll make the best of it", only to realise it's harmful for the other children to go through?

So, retreat to survival mode; do your resilience exercises if you have time. Just get through the day in one piece. Spend as much quality time with the other children as possible – indeed, insist on being fair(ish) with your time, even though on a bad day that'll have real consequences. They need to know they're special too. In due course they'll need to make their way out into the world in one piece, so you're always mindful of the need to minimise collateral damage. Generally, suck it up and deal with it. Official help is sporadic, disjointed, difficult to come by and often so poor as to be useless, but you remind yourself others have it far, far worse.

It's May 16th. I haven't even knocked on her door yet …

Name: Debbie Jenkins
Age: 52
Condition: Daughter's Obsessive Compulsive Disorder, Misophonia
Location: Manchester, United Kingdom

My life changed dramatically 16 years ago with the birth of my twin daughters. Then five years ago it changed again, this time beyond all recognition. Just after their 11th birthday, one of my twin daughters developed severely debilitating OCD. When I say debilitating, I mean paralysed in a way that most people can't comprehend. She couldn't move. Each single solitary movement could take hours and her level of distress was unbearable. Hospitalisation followed after three days of not eating. She simply couldn't get the food to her mouth. What happened is almost indescribable so I won't describe it. I genuinely feel words can't. What I can do is describe the aftermath for her, for the family and for me.

The road to recovery has been long; five years so far and we now know she has something else, something which is not even recognised here in the UK. It has a name: Misophonia. It sounds like a musical instrument – something pretty, but it's not. Like OCD, it causes havoc. It literally means 'hatred of sound', and it means my daughter can't even bear the sound of my voice as I am her main trigger and it evokes rage. Like OCD, a 'fight or flight' response, but often more 'fight' than 'flight', and it's not what I say but often just the words I use. Even psychiatrists believed she must

A Day in My Head

be angry with me but she's not and I quote, "Then they must be idiots. I don't hate you ... I just hate your voice!"

So now I have to be careful with everything I say. I have to stop talking if she gets stressed, even if I'm in another room of the house. Family outings are non-existent. There is an empty chair at the dinner table.

Going out becomes impossible so we don't go out together. It's not just my voice though, it's many other human sounds as well; for example, sniffing, swallowing, coughing. The things that we do every day - to her they are triggers and it makes day-to-day living almost impossible.

So back to today. How do I feel? Delicate. My lovely friend, in a well meaning chat, told me I had to think about how bad it could be. How bad other children were. At least she's not a school absentee, a drug addict, a teen mum, or worse, dead; but my beautiful, clever daughter spent nine months away from her family when she was so young, frightened because she didn't know what was happening to her. She has fought a hard, courageous yet invisible battle to get to where she is today. She is on the eve of her first formal exam but her future is uncertain, not like her twin sister who has choices, choosing how to spend the next few years; Chloe's choices are based on avoidance and anxiety. I know we shouldn't compare our children but how can I not when I KNOW that Chloe's choices would be so different without the spectre of Misophonia and OCD. So I worry obsessively (oh the irony). I sit at my PC and I search. I search for answers to her illness, search for treatment, search for support.

My great sadness is that we can't have a normal relationship. I can't even ask her how she is some days, so yes, it's great that she isn't any of those things my friend mentioned but why should we start from the worst possible place and be thankful we are not there? She should be able to go out with her family. Why don't people wonder where she is? It's all invisible. There is so much collateral damage. There is nothing funny about it even though some of my friends encourage me to see the humour. I know they are trying to help me and I know I should be grateful as they are the ones who understand as much as it is possible to understand, but how can they when we don't understand it ourselves – and worse, the medical profession, who should be helping us, don't 'get it' either. So tomorrow Chloe will take her first exam. She will do well; the teachers have predicted it, but what is the point of academic success if her most basic and important relationships are jeopardised and the world is inaccessible to her?

Name: Cathy Clarke
Age: 47
Condition: Obsessive Compulsive Disorder
Location: Greater Manchester, United Kingdom

Empathy, Coffee and OCD

When my Dad heard that I had OCD, he said very little at the time. I left his house wondering if telling him had been the right thing to do or just a foolish act of conscience. I guess what I wanted him to know was that some of my bizarre behaviours were not just quirks, but were the results of a debilitating condition.

I love my dad, I really love him. He is irreverent when he should be serious; serious when he should be comical. He has an answer for any question that I might ask and delivers a punchline with perfect rhythm and timing. He has a funny walk that he only shares with me and my sister and sings like a nightingale when the whiskey has loosened his vocal chords.

However, when I told him about OCD he did not have an answer for me or a solution. I felt a little lost.

Some days later, I accidentally read some notes that my dad had left next to his iPad. They were about OCD. The notes were detailed and were clearly well researched. There were columns on obsessions and compulsions, facts and statistics about incidence rates, helpline numbers and website addresses. At the bottom of the page were two words written in bold. One of these words was underlined and etched over several times for emphasis. That word was:

Empathy:

My dad knew me, but he still felt the need to write that word down because OCD is a condition that he did not understand or have all the answers to. However, not having the answer did not flaw him; he just reminded himself that to show empathy was a powerful, compassionate and necessary action.

The other word that he wrote in large letters on that crisp, white page was:

Coffee:

A Day in My Head

However, after the mitral valve diagnosis, he might have to settle for a decaf tea instead!

Cathy Clarke aka @caughtinaloop

Name: Aurora Kitaj
Age: 52
Location: Hackney, United Kingdom
Profession: Full Time Carer

After unstacking the dishwasher, prepared breakfast for son. At 6.45am, woke kids. With his breakfast, son takes Sertraline, an antidepressant he has been on for the last year. Sertraline has helped him to deal with low mood and depressive feelings. After breakfast, about 7am, son starts dressing. At age 15, it still takes him a while to dress in the mornings; he often gets sidetracked by more interesting things. Daughter at 13 is hampered a little by OCD rituals but manages to get dressed more quickly.

Realised with abject shock that son due to visit orthodontist in the centre of town today at 11:30am for initial assessment. Although this had been mentioned to him before the appointment had been made several months ago, had forgotten to remind him recently. The prospect of an appointment was additionally stressful, due to the requirement for teeth being ultra clean before his teeth can be assessed for braces. One of his lingering OCD rituals is around teeth cleaning. The compulsion associated with intensively cleaning his teeth can be to make himself sick.

8am: Dropped kids at school. The school they attend, whilst being tough on discipline and timekeeping, has taken a very flexible approach towards my son's difficulties. Indeed, without the support of his school, a high performing Academy, it's very unlikely that he would be able to be on roll now. Support staff have been painstakingly weaning him back into lessons over the last year. He became acutely ill with OCD last year and had to be admitted to adolescent psychiatric hospital for three months. We, all of us, have been venturing into uncharted territory since he was diagnosed a year and a half ago.

Arrive home. 8:30am: dispatched hurried email to orthodontic clinic, realising in all likelihood no notes would have accompanied the referral from dentist setting out his difficulties around brushing, particularly if there is a high expectation of flossing and cleaning!

Collect son at 9:15am from school. Followed by a little more surreptitious brushing and flossing. Next, to the bus stop followed by a complex set of interchanges involving bus and tube.

We arrive slightly early. Happily, orthodontist has read and understood my email. We learn that all is OK, he doesn't require braces. Buy sandwiches for lunch before visiting newly opened flagship bookstore, well-stocked with graphic novels, all to my sons taste.

On the return journey, leave son on bus to make his way back to school, something very happily he is now able to do. A year ago he would've been in hospital after OCD rendered him mute, incontinent, unable to leave his room, such were the terrible compulsions, rituals and intrusive thoughts that beset him. At that time, we could not a see a way forward, all our lives having been snatched away by OCD.

The day is not quite as stressful as it might have been had I still been working. Coping with OCD/Autism and working over the last few years would have been all but impossible on my own. Return home to emails and house work before leaving to collect kids at 3pm. On Thursdays, son attends an after-school club for disabled children. It is somewhere he has been visiting since not long after he was diagnosed with Autism in 2007. To us, Kids is like a second family who have been there when he has needed them. As with his school, I cannot speak too highly of the people who work there.

Back at home, watch daughter displaying her gymnastic trampoline skills in the back garden. The trampoline at home is an invaluable resource for both children: for my son to allow him to stim* and unwind after school, and for my daughter for much the same reason.

Collect son at 6pm from after-school club. Quite apart from this morning's dental visit, he has also been preparing for his GCSE drama exam this week. Perhaps inevitably, this has led to his worries about having missed so much school over the last year due to OCD; worries about being able to achieve GCSEs, A-levels, university entry and the risks of being long-term joblessness if he fails.

Son eats macaroni cheese for supper along with risperidone, and antipsychotic medication to help him unwind further at the end of the day. This drug usually just knocks him out.

*repetitive movements in autistic people

Name: Molly Collett
Age: 47
Condition: Son's Obsessive Compulsive Disorder
Location: Welwyn Garden City, United Kingdom

A Day in My Head

Today was a bad rituals day. Lots of left/right tapping. Josh has developed a strange walk recently – he drags his right foot behind him. He confided that this is due to having to manoeuvre past all parallel lines in a certain way; he has to pass parallel lines with his right foot last (or something like that – it all sounded very complicated when he tried to explain it to me). Practically everything around him has parallel lines so this is affecting his walking terribly.

At bedtime he had to do lots of left/right tapping on the pillow, certain tapping in a symmetrical way. While eating a bowl of grapes and cheese chunks, he couldn't touch a grape if it had already touched his mouth – if he did he had to go and do the hand-washing ritual again. I watched him eat a grape from the side of the bowl for some reason – he told me he couldn't touch the grape because it got "contaminated", but as a result the edge of the bowl was "contaminated," so if he accidentally touched it then he had to wash his hands again. He couldn't leave four grapes in the bowl as four and eight are particularly bad numbers at the moment. 8+4 is his worst sum at school he said. He showed me his hand washing ritual - he has to squirt soap then wash his hands then squirt soap and wash the tap, which may have been made dirty by someone else, then he has to squirt soap and wash his hands again as he's just touched a potentially dirty tap. He had to do this a number of times this evening, including after touching the grape which had already been "contaminated" with his own saliva.

I haven't been able to kiss my son goodnight, or goodbye, or good morning for months. Kissing is contamination.

He let me watch him do some other bedtime habits – he had to touch the wall 35 times (a hand counts as five). If he doesn't do it precisely in a certain way he has to start again. Then he confided something about parallel lines on his bedside chair and feet movements (too complicated for me to understand). About 10 minutes after his light was out he then confided that he had just finished another ritual which was left/right hand movements in the air of 35 x 15 times. So basically over 300 hand movements (something to do with imaginary parallel lines and moving his hands into them).

He told me that he doesn't want to have to do these habits but he can't feel good unless he does them. I reassured him that we were trying to get help.

Someone, please, please help us. It's getting worse, not better. He needs help. We all need help. I want to help him but don't know what else I can do. Why is this happening?

Name: Anna
Age: 45
Condition: Son's Obsessive Compulsive Disorder
Location: Cheshire, United Kingdom

I woke my son up this morning to take his usual medication – 200mg of Sertraline to treat his severe OCD, which is mainly linked to racial and sexual thoughts. He also has ASD and ADHD. He takes the Sertraline to help his OCD behaviours and mood.

Today, he would not have his shower until he had done his masturbating, which he does in multiples as this is a compulsion. He cleaned his teeth for the allocated time as usual. At the breakfast table he sat in the chair that he knew a non-Caucasian person that had recently visited, had not touched. He used the bathroom toilet rather than the downstairs one, which is now permanently 'contaminated' because a non-Caucasian person once used it. He procrastinated for ages before going into the shower as he knows he has many rituals to perform in there and he cannot face it.

After a lot of coaching, I got him into the shower. He started to wash repeatedly until it 'felt right'. It took about an hour today. He went to the toilet and shook his penis so many times until it 'felt right'. Then he washed his hands and wrists under the scalding hot water tap and cleaned them until they 'felt right' too. He put the fan on in the bathroom so he couldn't 'hear' the non-Caucasian person talking or moving at the back of our house. Muttering "there, there, there" under his breath to appease the OCD and to make him 'feel right'. No windows are allowed to be open whilst he is showering or washing or he will be contaminated by non-Caucasian people. He walked in between rooms whilst getting dressed and dried as many times as he needed to 'feel right'. He put his clothes on (he hates the feel of his clothes as they go across his body) as fast as possible so he didn't feel it! Occasionally OCD demands that he put the socks on again so many times or the t-shirt until it 'feels right'. Fortunately, this didn't happen today!

He turned on his computer as many times as he needed to 'feel right', as he knows that as soon as he starts gaming the OCD is a lot better. I had the TV on and he came downstairs to say that he can hear non-Caucasian voices and requested that I turn it off. I have to expose him to this feeling

A Day in My Head

of being uncomfortable and anxious by keeping the TV on and letting him stare at non-Caucasian people. He started to get wound up and snappy with me. I justified why I was exposing him to this and what I was trying to achieve, but it was hard for him to accept. This again set him off on compulsions for a while as he tried to counteract the 'non-Caucasian contamination'.

The doorbell rang and he froze. "Who is that, Mum? What colour are they? Are they non-Caucasian? Oh no, Dad will have to come home now!" Due to the non-Caucasian parcel delivery person he can do nothing until he sees a Caucasian male to counteract it. The day is ruined! The parcel and its contents are contaminated forever!

I rang the CAMHS department again as they hadn't returned my call. They said that my son is not "ill enough" to be transferred to Adult Services. I could feel my blood boiling as I have yet again got to go and complain to my useless MP that the Mental Health Services are letting us down. A three hour weekly outreach service for a fee of £25 a week is supposed to appease us instead so no therapy because apparently I can do that myself as a carer! I am met with a defensive stance from the care-coordinator, who says, "don't shoot the messenger – I don't make the decisions!" I asked who *does* make the decisions and could I speak to them instead, and he refused to give me their telephone number, insisting that he will get this person to ring me. I asked him if he was blocking me and he was very edgy. They didn't ring back, of course!

Watching my son ravaged by the OCD 'monster' is a painful experience. I fear for the future as I don't know whether he will ever be independent. My only outlet as a parent/carer is an OCD forum on Facebook with other long suffering parents ... this is my life!

To The Ends of the Earth

Focusing on the outside world. In so many ways, this is the greatest antidote to the recesses of mental ill health. "Stimulation. Excitement. The kind found in new places," advises Matt Haig, author of *Reasons to Stay Alive*. "By forcing yourself into a new physical space, preferably in a different country, you end up inevitably focusing a bit more on the world outside your head."

Name: Alexandra Valenzuela
Age: 27
Condition: Anorexia Nervosa
Location: Tokyo, Japan

Having moved to Japan, it is simultaneously great but also nerve-wracking. I'm exposed to many new and exciting things; however, I'm also so very far from family, friends and food comforts. In some ways, it's very liberating, not to be tied to the same old routine of skinny cappuccinos and 'safe' foods, but at the same time I do worry about getting bigger and not being aware of it. I am without access to 'skinny' milk, nor do I know what is in anything or how many calories are contained in the things I'm eating. Food can be a bit scary out here, and every now and then I get a wave of panic as to how much I'm eating, or how much I 'might' have eaten. The worst is when I deprive myself for a long period of time, I get panicky and can't make a simple decision, and from having been deprived for the day, eat to make up for the lack, and then end up feeling full and uncomfortable. I guess it's all about balance; eating when hungry and stopping when full, but when you don't trust yourself around food, this balance is easily upset.

I'm very 'over' food being an enemy; with a gluten intolerance too, it's hard to relax around food when you're in a culture that uses soy sauce (gluten alert!) in the way that the West use salt (which is on everything). Having a bad stomach makes me want to eat clean and reintroduce real, healthy foods, but high fat contents of very nutritious things is an excuse for me to put them back down on the shelf. I am enjoying exploring, but I do feel that this eating disorder locks me in a mindset of fearful anticipation; I worry that if I eat lunch, I'll not be hungry for dinner, or if I eat then I'm going to feel uncomfortably full. But most of the time, the reality is that when I eat when I'm hungry, I feel calmer, more energetic, generally good. It's just this fear that gets in the way and makes it complicated, and

A Day in My Head

whilst I know what is right for me, logic sometimes goes out the window.

I feel when I'm hungry that the obsessive and ruminative thoughts grow. Before I moved to Japan, I was blocking out the big, scary thoughts, like where am I going to live and how am I going to earn money, with obsession over details, such as 'where shall I get my morning coffee', and 'which is the lowest calorie dish on the menu?'. Of course, the logical me realises that this doesn't matter in the slightest, and a hearty lunch one day will have very little impact on my size, weight or general satisfaction in life over the next few months. But it's a way of grappling desperately for support or control in what is otherwise quite a chaotic existence.

Sometimes all I can fixate on is food, even after I've eaten it. I'm there, obsessing about which restaurant we go to, and which dish to get, and sometimes when someone is chatting to me I feel so overwhelmed I just need them to stop so I can have a moment of quiet in the otherwise busy mind of mine to make a decision that will keep both me, and my eating disorder, happy.

The waves of panic are occasional, much less now that I'm here in my space and zone than before I left London. It is like this terrifying jolt which I can only equate to when you suddenly realise you've lost your mobile phone; your stomach drops as you contemplate quite how many calories you think you've had, or as I look at the peanut butter jar and realised I've just manically stuffed half the thing in my mouth, in a frantic, starved manner.

I had dinner with my housemates the other day, which was actually really lovely. I still feel terrified by others judging me when I eat ('do I look like a pig?' 'Am I eating too much?' 'Do they think I'm disgusting?') I was quite pleased to see my housemate tucking in a very relaxed manner, getting sticky fingers and paying very little mind to my eating style, amount or manner. It seems that quirkiness is embraced here, which I think will be healthy for me.

Name: Portishead
Age: 22
Condition: Depression
Location: Breda, The Netherlands

Exactly one year ago, I fell really ill. Not the kind of illness which I could cure with some dab of ointments or a handful of paracetamols. Instead, I suffered from the invisible illness called depression without even realising it, and here is my story …

I had recently graduated from college and immediately moved to a foreign land, nearly four thousand miles away from my home. I went abroad to the UK to pursue my postgraduate studies in Philosophy, a subject that I loved deeply. The move was one of the biggest decisions that I had ever made and one for which I had been required to prepare myself both mentally and physically; to confront all challenges and difficulties, come what may.

Everything went smoothly for the first few months, with a few moments of homesickness every now and then. Though this genuinely did not worry me, as it was an obvious part of my journey to miss home, family and friends. Slowly and steadily, however, the pressure and stress of studies began to be felt more intensely.... And yet what else was I expecting? Stress and studies go hand in hand in every student's life. Although, in my case, the stress brought to me by the never-ending deadlines was perhaps much less significant than the stress I put on myself thinking about doing better in classes since my parents had invested so much financially in making my dream come true.

As days passed by, I started feeling more and more upset and sad, spending my days and nights worrying incessantly about the need to perform better in classes. It didn't take long for my worries to turn into this colossal feeling of guilt about how I might have wasted my parent's hard earned resources, which in turn lead to me questioning my love for the subject, as well as my decision to move abroad. From there on, my control over how I felt was seemingly no longer in my own hands. Things were starting to descend in a spiral-like momentum which could only end in a final state of me feeling depressed every single day.

However, back then I had not realised what had actually triggered this chain of events. I don't have the answer even today. It was not the case that my grades were falling. To the contrary, I was doing well in classes. It was not the case that my parents were disappointed in me. No, they couldn't be more proud of me than they already were. What, why, how – I still don't know. When I look back, the only flashbacks that I have are of me locking myself in my six square meter room, laying in my bed all day with the grim grey skies of England as the only scenery from my window. I can remember those untimely, inexplicable outburst of tears, that dying desire to feed or care for myself, those dark thoughts of the apparently miserable life I had.

A Day in My Head

But the most hurtful feeling was that of not being in control of my emotions. The deadly combination of feeling helpless and lost, without being surrounded with my family, and the urgent need to finish my studies on time with good grades – I would never ever wish for such an experience again. Had I known what exactly was happening to me and had I taken the steps to speak to my parents or colleagues or even a doctor about what I was going through, I might have saved myself from spending the entire year in this mental jail.

Somehow, I managed to survive those days, submitted my masters thesis and instantly booked a flight back home. I started consulting with a therapist and did all that I could to lead a happier life. I hope that after reading this small excerpt from my life, many would be able to relate and help someone who is going through the same.

Name: Avadhoot Shejwalkar
Age: 19
Condition: Primarily Obsessional Obsessive Compulsive Disorder (Pure-O OCD)
Location: Pune, Maharashtra, India

It was quite early when I woke up to the sound of rain pouring down on muddy, concrete roads outside my apartment; when I thought that I wasn't myself but had being changed into a friend of mine. These kind of thoughts are some of the many obsessions I have. The compulsions vary from rethinking the thoughts and converting them into 'good' ones, to touching the objects I would have been touching whilst obsessing. Though, in truth, the kind of compulsions and obsessions don't really matter …

At the time of writing, I am diagnosed with primarily obsessional OCD – or Pure O – targeted toward mental contamination and harm thoughts. This is not a perfect diagnosis, but it is sufficient.

So anyway, back to my day – I have recently finished all the entrance exams, and though they didn't go quite as well as I would have liked because of my OCD, I don't waste time thinking about it. Note that I am also a chaotic, good INTP; a personality type, pretty rare, which involves not only unique creativity but also a tendency to get lost in abstractions. I am certain that this often feeds into my symptoms of OCD.

After performing compulsions a few times, I get up and start to freshen up. My obsessions 'haunt' me constantly while brushing, bathing, and while talking to my parents at breakfast. I don't have a plan to execute during the day and so I start to use my computer, a session which enables me to at least partly ignore the obsessions. After programming for about a couple of hours, I sit back and rest, whilst continuing to tackle OCD, of course . As part of ERP treatment, I decide to ignore all obsessions for 30 mins. Well, I succeed at ignoring about 80% of them and sweating lots in the process. Most of the time, I am lost in my thoughts. Fortunately on this occasion, I refer to the random thoughts I have, which do not include intrusive thoughts ...

It is very much in my nature to contemplate anything and everything, ranging from science to philosophy about life. I am an atheist and fairly nihilistic. Note that this does enable me to ignore my thoughts more easily, though it is not a given remedy by any stretch. As intrusive thoughts begin to infiltrate my perfect imaginative world I begin to panic that I may lose the amazing and beautiful world in my mind where I can get lost for what seems like ages. I start to give in to compulsions and my anxiety rises. I can manage to calm myself after about five minutes and reduce the compulsions. It is difficult for me to actually stop the obsessions. They are involuntary and are mostly auditory but can become visual.

I decide to watch my favourite anime *Death Note* by Tsugumi Ohba-san to get lost again in my imaginary world. I am much like Eru Roraito from *Death Note* in many ways. I used to be ashamed of having OCD, but nowadays I don't mind it because my OCD has enabled me to think about things more rationally. It does sound paradoxical but it reduces the unnecessary things people tend to cling on to from one's life. I wouldn't give up my OCD because it has lead to me gaining information about a lot of stuff which has changed my perspective about so much. Though, please don't think that I am optimistic about my condition because I am not in the least. Nor am I really a pessimist. It's just that I have a really bad opinion of human emotions and their effects on reasoning. It makes me angry to see that I can't come to the most logical conclusion in the midst of an argument or a complex situation due to emotional involvement in the matter ...

I have been suffering from OCD now for two years but I told my parents about it only three months ago and got diagnosed at the same time. After watching anime for about four hours, I read scientific journals on the internet without giving in to OCD for about two hours. Then I proceed to sleep. I manage to sleep for three hours after a struggle with intrusive thoughts. I speak with my girlfriend for about two hours on the phone and then I spend my time till dinner programming. I have dinner with my parents and my

A Day in My Head

OCD, after which I rest and proceed to sleep. I think about how disabled my OCD has made me. Overall on the OCD scale, today was 5/10. Peace out.

Name: Nora Alghaslan
Age: 32
Condition: Depression
Location: Doha, Qatar
Profession: Founder of *Consciousness Connected*

As a multicultural person, it has been a struggle to live in a country like Saudi Arabia, due largely to the conservative culture. People are not encouraged to think or to question, and even though I am a Saudi woman I have been raised to be an independent thinker. However, having lived in such an environment, it has definitely put a lot of pressure on my mental well-being. And even though the struggles were many, such as relentless gender discrimination, I always managed to get back up and move on. Yet in the light of my last traumatising experience of being physically abused several times by my younger brother, shunned, rejected and forced out of my country by my biological family (excluding my father), just because I openly and sometimes aggressively expressed that I would not tolerate double standards due to my gender, things had finally collapsed around me. After having left Saudi Arabia, I was forced to face the internal issues that I have been unwittingly avoiding for so long.

The depression and anxiety became a full-blown disorder and I have been battling it for over two years now, but with the help of family (not my immediate family) friends, a doctor, and medication, I was able to get rid of my anxiety and am yet healing my depression. I have had to undergo a very challenging grieving process, which has finally lead me to acceptance and forgiveness. Now, here comes the amazing part. When we go through painful experiences and we are able to heal, this becomes the motivation that will drive us to our life's purpose. Due to this very painful experience, I was able to finally find the courage to trust myself and open up to the world, like a blossoming flower. Now, I have created a non-profit organisation, whose goal is to help others open up to their potential through gaining spiritual knowledge and understanding of the self and the universal laws of unity.

Today is a good day because I woke up with a smile on my face – but it's not always the case. As I continue to recover and treat my depression, some days are better than others and today seems to have started quite well. I have noticed that one of the best cures for me is when I keep myself engaged and focused on what I love, which is writing, working on evolving my non-profit organisation, and music. However, there are days when I still feel like my heart is being ripped apart, but I push through it, which makes me feel better, giving me the energy to continue to do what I love. Because depression kills the will to do even the things we love; who would not want to do the things they love unless they were truly unwell?!

Depression can be a lifelong illness, and one way to deal with it is to accept its existence and to work with it. In my case, I notice that the more I accept it and go with the flow while continuing my treatment, the longer the time between episodes, as well as the shortening of each episode. Acceptance and patience are key to dealing with any disorder, no matter how hard – and it can be extremely hard. That's why the community must be educated in how people who suffer from a mental illness need love, support and understanding, just like anyone with a physical ailment, such as high blood pressure or cardiovascular disease.

I do hope that more people become aware of the importance of addressing such issues, and that people with mental illness have qualities that may be beneficial, such as empathy and sensitivity, which can direct them to a more constructive path. However, as long as mental illness is stigmatised, leading those who suffer from it into isolation instead of seeking help, society will never benefit from what these individuals would otherwise have to offer in their own unique way.

Name: Bernadine Tan (Nadine)
Age: 25
Condition: Anxiety
Location: Cainta, Calabarzon, Philippines

I don't think my story is remarkable but I believe every story is unique. And even though I was running out of motivation to write, Mr. Aron still encouraged me to continue. So here it goes:

I am Bernadine Tan, or Nadine for short. I'm from Philippines (I did not include the "the" because it bothers me so – haha), and I'm currently a 25-year old employee in a finance institution.

My weekday starts as early as 4:30 in the morning: taking a shower, dressing for work and travelling with my brother in our three-box

A Day in My Head

sedan to the business district. It takes us about an hour and thirty minutes to get to our respective office buildings.

The day, as usual, passes by without anything out of the ordinary. It is plain routine to perform my function as a secretary and as a support staff to the department. At the end of my shift, I hurriedly proceed to the drive and fetch my brother at his office. The journey back home takes much longer; sometimes as much as 45 minutes extra because of the rush hour traffic. But when we get home, the exhaustion from working and the terrible traffic jam is compensated by our enthralled pets, eager to welcome us. It is a relief to see them.

After dinner, only a few hours might be spent browsing the net or reading a book. This is followed finally by waiting patiently for sleep to come and lull me to a deep rest, in preparation for another work day.

It is only during weekends that I get a complete rest and a break from the monotony of my work.

As you see, monotony has been the theme of my life now. It may seem dull to others. As for me, I don't know where my life is heading to right now. After I graduated from college, my motivation seems slowly to have diminished. Whatever it was that I was aiming for when I was studying, has been lost in sight over the five years that I have been working. The drive that's been pushing me to go farther and to improve myself, has been taken over by the mediocre satisfaction and aimless state of mind over the years that I've been working. I thought that maybe the hopelessness and dullness was caused by the burnout, or my colleagues, or maybe the stress and pressure, not only from the office, but from the everyday customary routine that I've been going through. Perhaps it was my cowardice; wanting to seek out the things that I haven't yet explored but being too scared to go through with it. I am nervous of the things that could jeopardize everything that I have already established and believed in. But sometimes change is what we need to find what we are really looking for. To find what I am really looking for. And change is what could get us to our rightful destinations.

I am already 25 and I am not getting any younger. There's still time to change and aim for something to give my life meaning and purpose but time itself can be an enemy, as well as an ally. Nevertheless, if we really are determined to change for the better, to get ourselves where we are meant to be, whatever hurdles or obstacles the circumstances may engender, our "why" should always give us the drive to continue our path; to improve ourselves and achieve the change that we are looking for. And unconsciously, along the way, we are given, in my humble view, just enough time and opportunities to reach what we are aiming for.

I hope all of us would find our "why" sooner before time has passed us by, for it would help us to work together for the betterment of everyone, not only here but across the entire world. Let us pray for each other so that we may endure whatever life may throw at us. For every human being's life in this world is precious and life itself is worthwhile.

Always remember to think of others, for genuine love is an act of selflessness. Take care!

Name: Kelly Wilson
Age: 40
Condition: Depression, Anxiety, and Post-Traumatic Stress Disorder
Location: Portland, Oregon, United States
Profession: Author and Comedian

Dear Diary,

Sometimes my depression, anxiety, and posttraumatic stress disorder make me want to stay in bed all day.

Today was not one of those days. Today I was ready for an outdoor adventure.

I knew it was going to be a good day when I "played possum" for almost an hour, fooling my family into thinking that I was still asleep as they went about their morning business. My body announces that I'm awake each morning by farting out all the air trapped by my sphincter during the night. The farting is so good but sometimes I don't want everyone to know I'm awake right away. This morning I was practicing Mindful Farting (TM), which allows the air to escape with a minimum of noise (let's be honest, I do enjoy my anal melodies). Success! Husband remained convinced that I was still sleeping until I sauntered into the living room where he had already made the coffee.

With little on my calendar and beautiful sunlight assaulting my senses, I decided it was time for a hike to nearby Steins Pillar. I had never been there, but the photos were beautiful and the hike was described as "easy".

A Day in My Head

After two miles on a gravel off-road I arrived at the trailhead, only to find no toilet of any kind. Though by this point, the throb of my bladder was merely a whisper and the "easy" trail was but two miles long, one way. Surely there would be plenty of places to pee as my urge became more insistent ...

Oh diary, the start of the hike was as rough as the rocky soil beneath my feet. I silently cursed the guidebook. How is this hike "easy?" Did the author of my guidebook happen to hike with Jesus, and the Lord himself declared, "Why yes, this trail is, in fact, 'easy.'" Did the author forget that he was hiking with Jesus, who spent like a month and a half in the frickin' desert on a vision quest? I guess compared to climbing Mt. Everest, this trail could be considered easy.

After about ten minutes, my body and mind resigned themselves to moving forward, uphill both ways, of course. I searched in vain for a place off the trail to relieve my bladder as I hiked to the top. Though surrounded by giant boulders, scrub, open vistas, ravines, and sharp hillsides, there were no sheltered areas as I continued to climb.

After throbbing for an hour and almost reaching the top of the Steins Pillar hike, I eventually found it; a veritable oasis for full-bladdered hikers. Facing the trail, this bladder harbor was walled in all three sides with dense brush and trees.

Angling over the ground, I peed for forty seconds straight, praying that no snakes strike my vulnerable undercarriage. I had unknowingly positioned myself over a small, knobby branch, which spewed my forceful pee back up onto me, my socks, my shoes ... all the while a bird cawed insistently about my presence. I became convinced this bird called for his pecking pals
to eat my eyes. And I would be found by hikers, eyeless and covered in my own urine.

Eager to escape the bird, I did not take time to shake before pulling up my shorts. In just a couple of switchbacks, I made it to the top of the hike. My eyes feasted on the glorious surroundings, and I felt my spirit lift. I hunted in my backpack for my two bottles of water I had prepared for my trip to sip while enjoying the view I had laboured so hard to see.

They were gone. As in, dear diary, I had forgotten to pack them. I perched on a boulder, my anxiety ramping up, envisioning a slow death from dehydration in 70 degree heat on top of this mountain.

There was nothing left to do but make my way back down the trail. Plus, the wind was really whipping up, chilling my damp nether region.

I lumbered back down the two miles to the trailhead. Sweat dripped into my eyes. I probably should have held my pee until the end of the hike, so maybe my body could absorb all of that liquid and avoid dehydration. That's a thing, right?

The sandy trail became my nemesis as it wound through scrub and forest and along ravines. With a steep hillside on one side and a rocky, tree-filled ravine on the other, my foot slipped on the sandy trail. I would have peed my pants in fear, as I slid onto my backside, one leg out and the other bent.

I landed between two rocks, my arms across their tops as if I sat on a throne. Diary, this little throne saved me from tumbling down the ravine and probably dying a terrible death. I hadn't even been thinking about suicide ideation and I might have died.

Diary, I ask you, what kind of irony would that be?

The Case for Optimism

Where there's life, there is hope. These words from Stephen Hawking, beautifully recaptured in James Marsh's *Theory of Everything*. Even Nietzsche, that former pessimist, understood, in the end, the inherent, osmotic relationship between pain and art, as well as the importance of 'self-overcoming'. And nowhere do we see a greater example of this than in the rich, highly literate contributions made to this project by our one hundred writers, some of whom are chronicling the very worst psychological turmoil...

Name: Catlin A. Palmer
Age: 29
Condition: Obsessive Compulsive Disorder, Anxiety
Location: San Diego, California, United States
Profession: Social Worker and CEO of Life Coaching Business

I'm struggling to get out of bed ... just like any other weekday morning. As I am slowly trying to wake up and let my eyes adjust and focus, my mind sparks into hyper-mode, which is quite normal for me. Although I would describe the intensity of the emotions and thoughts racing through my mind as not so normal. Especially at 7am when I haven't even had a chance to get out of bed yet. These extreme thoughts flood my mind in the mornings and generally trigger the beginning to my daily ongoing battle with OCD and anxiety.

About three years ago I was diagnosed with OCD, Anxiety (Social Phobia), and Depression. Later I dealt with addiction and self-medicating issues with street drugs as well. The OCD causes my mind to drag me to places that I don't want to go, which almost always leads to anxiety. I have begun to learn that a great counter to this is to find three things I am grateful for. Every morning, I count three different things I am grateful for, which helps to push back on my mind's attempt to initiate anxiety. Gratitude is the attitude, as they say ... I truly believe in that as I have found being more grateful has helped decrease my mental ill-health symptoms. To be grateful or to be aware of the positives in your life sets you up for success because of the framework your mind begins to work in. Rather than always succumbing to the negatives that our mind can't help to throw in our face, we can better spend our time focusing on what *is* good, no matter how little there is to be proud of or happy about.

Currently, I am a social worker for a healthcare company in San Diego, CA. I graduated with a Master's Degree in Social Work in 2011 and have been happily working in the industry for the last five years. As I get ready for work, I can't help but to notice my mind nagging at me about anything and everything. Do not take the words "anything" and "everything" lightly, as my mind knows no bounds. While brushing my teeth I'm contemplating how terribly disconnected everybody seems to be in the world nowadays. My mind can't help but to wonder about the negative effects these types of things will have on the human race. In other words, how many more deaths do there need to be for the world to realize that we all are in this together and that the sooner we begin to love each other, the sooner we can save this planet ... and this is all going on in my head before 8am. Yes I know, these are things that are, for the most part, very much out of my control; however, that's also not to say that thinking these things doesn't have a negative emotional effect on me. What I need to remember is I must continue being positive, hopeful, and optimistic about my own individual life. It all hearkens back to a saying by Ghandi that I will never forget, "Be the change you wish to see in the world." This quote makes so much sense because not any single individual can necessarily change the whole entire world at once, but in changing the one thing they can absolutely control – themselves – they are then, in a sense, taking the first steps to changing the world.

The amount of words I can write is very limited so I will lightly summarize the rest of my day. I work my eight hours as usual. Afterwards, I hit the gym (three or four times a week). The gym takes precedence over almost anything else in my life. I did not set out to create that intention, but I have found over the last 10 years that going to the gym isn't something I necessarily want to do as much as it is something I *need* to do. The physical exertion and mental stamina working out has been one of the best symptom management tools throughout my recovery.

I am a Life Coach, so if you have any further interest in my journey please take a moment to check out my website (www.flowmentum-movement.com). The newsletters contain free information and valuable tips on overcoming our mind and how to be happy right now while still pursuing our dreams.

Name: Christine Roberts
Age: 57
Condition: Bipolar Disorder
Location: Washougal, Washington, United States

A Day in My Head

When I woke up today I felt pretty good. First, I think of all I have to do for the day. I seem to have a routine that keeps me stable. This is important. I have several Bipolar Disorder orientated groups that I have created, so first thing this morning I get online and catch up on them.

It happens that I, too, live with Bipolar Disorder. Specifically, I have Bipolar I/Manic Disorder. The psychotic symptoms and/or tendencies I get during mania episodes include schizophrenia, paranoia and delusions, which, I am always keen to highlight, are different from hallucinations. I was first hospitalized when I was a little over seventeen and a half, and off and on, in and out of hospital, for going on 40 years now. Back then of course, there was no such diagnosis as Bipolar Disorder and it was thought that I suffered a drug overdose and would not come out of it. It wasn't until I was about 34 years old that I was properly diagnosed. I'm 57 years old now and have less severe manic episodes, but still suffer with mood swings and the intense emotions that go along with the disorder. I haven't been hospitalized in several years now. I take anti-psychotic medications, pills for mania, and an anti-depressant to help manage the disorder.

I know for me it's really important to keep taking my meds regularly as prescribed. I am on medication management with my psychologist and I see a nurse for my treatment plan. My son is a nurse and is in charge of my medication management at home. Before that, when I was doing it by myself, I'd be okay for a while but during my manic episodes I would forget and take too much, and then have to be hospitalized for a toxic dose. I am pleased to say I've been stable now for the last five months and haven't been this well, self-aware, and with such a positive state of mind for about 40 years!

There are other things that have helped too (alongside medication adjustments and the eventual withdrawal from any form of 'recreational' drugs and alcohol). I have joined a couple of groups in my church, one for crocheting prayer shawls and the other for bible study. I also watch Major League Baseball while crocheting. I do some volunteer work for one of the Pastors at church (that I might get done today, with any luck), which I find immensely satisfying.

If there is perhaps one thing I feel I must hammer home then it is this: if it wasn't for the right medication and dosage I wouldn't be where I am today with my mental health. I'm a firm believer that, despite often contrary opinions, professional or otherwise, it is the management of one's medication that is the key to managing Bipolar Disorder. I urge anyone suffering with this disorder to hang on in there and to keep on trying to find the right balance for them. It will be worth it in the end.

Name: TravelingBPD
Age: 29
Condition: Borderline Personality Disorder
Location: München, Germany

Where shall I start? A day in my head surely is a roller coaster ride. Every day. I can never know what waits around the corner. Which feeling will attack me next. Which mood is going to surprise.

But it's not just these little changes, mood swings, outbursts and waves that I have to keep up with. It also goes deeper. With BPD I can find myself one minute believing in me, in what I do, in my plans, in who I'm with, in what I want, in what I like, and then next, out of nowhere I start to doubt everything. I'm no longer sure of anything. Everything falls apart.

I constantly have to fight with words in my head. There never seems to be a cease fire. My brain keeps on firing at me; one moment its doubts and thoughts about other people making fun of me without *any* objective indication for that. My head keeps on bringing up old pictures, words, situations that happened ages ago. So, of course, there is no chance of doing anything about it. But still my brain keeps on presenting those things to me.

Being around other people is always a difficult thing for me and my head. I'm a high functioning Borderliner, so I would never shout or scream at other people (who are not my boyfriend), even if my whole being feels like doing exactly that. Instead of letting it out, I keep those things inside. And not just things like anger. But also helplessness, hopelessness, desperation, self-criticism. They build up until the tension is too big to be held inside. Until it lets itself out. And most often this happens via self-harming behaviour.

I am now fortunate enough to be in recovery. Nevertheless, all of this is still everyday life for me, even after months of treatment and effort and work. But it's better; my head is no longer the winning party 24/7. Or, it still is, but not constantly the negative, downgrading, fighting, nagging, broken parts. These days, the positive, the good, the loving side of my head has a chance, too.

Rationality has a chance to sit behind the wheel, as has understanding, patience and self-care. Through Dialectic Behavioral Therapy (DBT), I have learned to cope with many of the things my disorder throws at me. I have learned to not just listen to my head, but to question the words and thoughts it produces. I have learned that I need to give myself attention, to care about me. This is still

A Day in My Head

hard, as I am still not really fond of myself. But I am fond of my body. How it's working every day to keep me alive. The things it had to endure for years – constantly destroying it with drugs and razors. I have learned that I want to take care of all the cells that I am made of.

Mindfulness and meditation gave me the tools to work with my head. To be able to not be defenceless and at its mercy all the time. That I have the power to influence what I think, how I think and, through this, ultimately how I feel. These days, I take extra care of the body I was given and of the things that go on in my head. Both my body and my head need training; both are susceptible to breaks.

I have learned that when I take good care of my body, my brain also profits. When I manage to sleep enough, eat healthily, don't drink, work out, meditate and feel from the *inside* what I truly need, then my head gets more relaxed. The constant attacks are not that often and not that powerful anymore. Instead of constantly avoiding my own head, I have the energy, the skills and the strength to work with it.

So, a day in my head used to be 100% bad, exhausting, negative, depressing and all the other bad words you can think of. But now, a day inside my head can still be some of that, but there are also moments of happiness, joy, relaxation, hope and all the other good things you can think of. And it's *me* who decides how my head works.

Name: Olivia Bamber
Age: 24
Condition: Obsessive Compulsive Disorder
Location: London, United Kingdom
Profession: Media and Communications officer at OCD Action

October 2011
"I get into bed and spend the rest of the day there. It's times like these I don't want to be here – it's too hard to cope and I can't even begin to think about doing Uni work. Despite a close friend assuring me that being uncomfortable is the first step to getting better, I feel horrid and hopeless. I wish I was someone else."

May 2016
It's difficult to picture the person writing those words, filled with such despair that the only thing they could do was curl up and sleep.

I wrote those words five years ago in my OCD journal, a journal in which I documented my deepest thoughts and feelings about my OCD, at a time when I couldn't even get dressed on my own, and had hundreds of thoughts and rituals a day…

"I pick up my towel for the bathroom with one finger because I can't get my hands clean after touching the carpet. I wouldn't put my towel in the bathroom though because the rail is dirty. I wash my hands when I get out of the shower because I turned the shower on with dirty hands. After getting dry with a hairdryer I wash my hands again and then change my clothes again because they are wet, as I haven't dried myself properly. I fill the dishwasher then wash my hands because a cup I put in I had used when my hands were dirty. I put a tea bag in the bin then wash my hands because the bin lid is gross. I baby-wipe my phone and then wash my hands again because I touched my phone after touching the carpet. I just put the heater on and it smelt funny so now I'm going to have to shower again because I will smell."

Reading this back, I feel like I've picked up a book of fiction. My emotions range from shock, to sadness, to pure disbelief that my own brain could have made me feel that low by consuming with doubts and fears. I flick forward a few months…

December 2011

"My New Year's Resolution is to get this OCD under control finally. I recently had an amazing three days fairly OCD free. I want my whole life to be like those three days."

May 2016

It might have taken me more than a year to accomplish that New Year's Resolution, and realistically it's probably the only one I have ever stuck to, but I did it. I sought help, a lot of help, which once I was too ashamed to ask for. It was the best thing I ever did. I don't recognise the girl who wrote in that diary. Instead of waking up and my first thought being filled with fear and upset, I wake up and think of the episode of *The Walking Dead* I watched the night before, or what dress I plan on wearing at the weekend – the sort of things I should be thinking aged 25. I still get the same thoughts, though nowhere near as often, but with good therapy I have learnt how to react to them differently. It's not always easy and there is work to be done, but generally I enjoy a day in my head now, instead of being controlled by it. I've kept the journal; it's a strong

A Day in My Head

reminder for me that OCD can get better, for anyone, no matter how much it makes you feel otherwise.

Name: LM
Age: 32
Condition: Depression
Location: London, United Kingdom

By coincidence, today was the first day back at work after having been off for mental health reasons. I was quite scared this morning. I knew the best thing for me would be to go in, to be positive and productive rather than get more behind, more stressed, feel worse. But it just seemed so hard. It was so tempting to just hide from it all. I pictured myself climbing out the window in my pyjamas to escape. When I was absent, I'd self-harmed because I felt guilty for not being there for the children I supported, who also self-harm. This was ridiculous. And then I instinctively called out in pain, inadvertently trying to do the washing-up in scolding dish water. To complain about unexpected pain when I'd just deliberately hurt myself was ludicrous. But I went back to work today and I got through it. It went okay. My hands no longer look like I've shoved them in a bunch of stinging nettles. I did some planning for a project where older children befriend younger ones. I ate cake, I chatted with my colleagues. I came home to my lovely husband. I'll try again tomorrow.

Name: Kaye McLaren
Age: 58
Condition, Depression, Suicidal Ideation
Location: Wellington, New Zealand

How I Transformed Chronic Depression into Lasting Happiness

I wake up naturally, for the first time in many months, thanks to the new earplugs my friend gave me. I wonder if today I'm going to be well enough to go out, or whether I'll be stuck inside all day like yesterday. I have the meeting of my ME/CFS group today and really want to go. I feel good. I'm looking forward to today, to seeing people I like, hopefully, and to a walk with my dogs. My illness, the noisy, inconsiderate neighbours, the fact that I'm living in my lounge so I can rent out my bedroom and pay off debts, don't really matter that much. I'm happy.

It wasn't always like this. More days than I can remember I woke up to become aware of the grinding pain of depression. From that first moment of awareness I would start to fantasise - repetitively, obsessively - about killing myself. I wanted to so much. Only my work gave me a reason to keep living. Starting with Major Depressive Disorder, the relapses and suicidal periods went on for 12 years. But now I've been happy for most of the last 20 years. All the skills I learnt, all the new habits I developed, have paid off.

These days I use around 50 different techniques to keep my mood in a good place. I plan my day, do enjoyable activities, see people I like, write down the good things, exercise, spend time in nature, get bright light, eat fruit and vegetables every day, work on goals that are meaningful to me, reframe negative situations, focus on the positive, watch funny videos online and do other things to build my positive emotions.

If I feel down I write about my thoughts and look for the logical and factual errors in them, and correct them. I don't do this too often as I don't enjoy it much, but it's a good skill to have when I need it. I *don't* meditate! I find that way too boring. But I pay attention to my emotions, sensations and surroundings, and focus on the things I like, accept the rest. Every so often I write down a fantasy of how my life might be in the future if everything goes well.

Today I don't have time to write down good things or do much apart from some essential chores before I go out. But I have my plan, I have things to look forward to, and I'll spend time having fun and being social. I have also planned exercise in a lovely cemetery surrounded by huge trees. I have my piece of fruit before breakfast and I'll have my veggies with dinner. Throughout the day I automatically notice and accept my emotions.

This is the bedrock of my happiness process. Whether I am depressed, anxious, angry, desperate – and believe me, I still feel all of these emotions at times – I accept them, name them, feel them, even luxuriate in them. Then I go on with my planned day. This is what keeps me on the planet. If I suppress my negative feelings they go underground and take me under with them.

I make it to my support group, and have a wonderful time chatting, laughing and eating, even though I have to spend half the time there lying down. Then I walk my dogs, enjoying the winter sun and the huge trees. As I do all these things I feel content, relaxed. I'm not euphoric, but it feels fine to be me. I wish I could go back and tell that poor, desperate, miserable woman how good life can be, if she

A Day in My Head

just doesn't give up. I am glad that I survived the two suicide attempts. I wouldn't go as far as saying I'm glad I'm alive, but I'm OK with it. I have goals, activities I enjoy, friends, meaning, laughter and light in my life.

When I get home I go straight to bed, even though it's only 5pm. I spend sixteen to twenty-three hours a day in bed – today was a good day, only 17 hours. I'm excited about going on Twitter and Facebook, chatting with friends, having a yummy dinner. I don't dread being awake or long for sleep as I did so many evenings in the past. I'm comfortable with myself, I enjoy most of what I do and my own company. Life is good.

Name: Rebecca Lombardo
Age: 43
Condition: Bipolar Disorder
Location: Framington, Michigan, United States.
Profession: Published Author

I was nineteen years old when I was diagnosed with bipolar disorder. From that point on, life was a struggle. My moods were up, down, and back up again. I never knew what to expect. In my late twenties, I decided that I wanted to take my life. In the end, I just couldn't do it.

However, I did succeed in teaching myself how to use self-injury as a coping mechanism.

After being committed on two separate occasions and losing every job I ever had, I had no clue where my life was headed. I would date here and there, and inevitably I was dumped because of my illness. Relationships with horrible people that abused me soon followed. By the grace of God, I met the man who would eventually be my husband, and we were married in August of 2001. He was there for me when nobody else would take the risk. In 2006, we moved into our first home and things seemed to be looking up.

Life changed drastically when my mom was diagnosed with lung cancer in September of 2007. I promised her I would be at her side for everything, and I was. She passed away in January of 2008, and my life fell to pieces. I was filled with grief that I was unable to overcome. March 23, 2011, was my birthday. It seemed like any other day until I got a phone call from my dad. I thought it was a "happy birthday" call, but what he said made my legs buckle. One of my brothers had died and I never got to say goodbye.

In 2013, my husband and I were very happy. Until that summer when the depression hit me like a brick. Overwhelmed by sadness and grief, I decided it was time to go. I missed my mom and my brother immensely. I couldn't cope with my life any longer. I cut myself repeatedly and took a full bottle of one of my medications. I sat on the floor and sobbed. My husband was at work, but via text message he sensed something was very wrong. When he got home, he took me to the emergency room. I stayed in the hospital on suicide watch for five days. I was then told that the state was having me committed.

They strapped me to a gurney and hauled me off by ambulance to the most God forsaken place I have ever seen. I spent the next four terrible days locked away in that place with violence, threats, and no medical treatment whatsoever.

Walking out of there, I knew my life had to change. I swore never to take another razor blade to my skin. I promised myself that I would never put my husband or my family through any of that again. I decided that if I told my story, it might help people. By helping others, I knew I would be helping myself. I began writing a blog detailing all of my struggles, and eventually it became a book.

I am now a month shy of three years clean from self-injury. My writing has been the best therapy I have ever known. I'm extremely proud to be able to say that I'm now a published author. People reach out to me every day to say thanks.

Even though my life is much better, I need to be realistic. I will never be cured, and medication will forever be a part of my life. I am OK with that. If anyone I know isn't, I don't need them in my life. I'm taking care of myself for the first time. I've lost a lot of friends and even family members because of my suicide attempt. There are people that consider me selfish.

I'm here to tell you that suicide has nothing to do with being selfish. Having bipolar disorder doesn't make you selfish. Allowing yourself to find happiness doesn't make you selfish. I'm 43 years old, and I'm living proof that you can succeed despite your disability. It will take a lot of work, and you will stumble more often than you sprint. It can be done. Just take the first step.

A Day in My Head

Name: Katlyn Hashway
Age: 19
Condition: Obsessive Compulsive Disorder, Depression
Location: Hendersonville, North Carolina, United States

Having obsessive compulsive disorder, little things often make me incredibly anxious. This was more than apparent whilst checking my emails this morning. I opened my inbox to an email from my therapist, explaining that she'd contacted someone who triggers my OCD. She wants me to call him in order to make me anxious. To anyone unfamiliar with exposure and response prevention therapy, this probably doesn't sound therapeutic. It sounds cruel. However, exposure therapy changed my life.

OCD is a disorder characterized by repetitive intrusive thoughts. The thoughts are terrifying to the sufferer, so they respond with a mental or physical compulsion to neutralize the anxiety surrounding the thoughts. The problem is, doing compulsions to avoid the anxiety only ever makes the thoughts come back stronger. So the sufferer ends up stuck with these terrifying thoughts and the only thing they can think of that may help them is in reality only making them worse …

There was a time when I was controlled by my thoughts. However, through exposing myself to the thoughts and not doing compulsions, I took my life back from OCD. Although some symptoms still remain.

OCD is a treatable disorder, but it is a sticky disorder. Therefore, treatment must be sticky too. It's a process, but I've come to appreciate it. Exposing myself to my fear means I can live life the way *I* want to, not the way my OCD would have it. I want to see this person who makes me anxious because I like them. Therefore, I will, despite my anxiety.

The call my therapist wants me to make is preparation for when I actually see this person. I know avoiding the anxiety only makes it worse, so I'm standing up to it now. Like a bully on the playground, it will run away crying. As for today, I knew it would be useless to ruminate over what will happen when the person calls back. Therefore, I continued today's plans as usual.

My mom recently found a new clothing store, so we decided to go there. Afterwards, my parents and I stopped at a couple of stores to look at laptops. Unfortunately, mine recently decided to break as I was working on a video project. After returning from shopping, my dad and I drove to my grandmother's house.

It's important for me to do things and not stay curled up in bed all day. Although it's easy for me to become a bit of a recluse, being a recluse only serves to make me depressed. For some reason, doing something fun when I'm depressed, even when I don't want to, makes me feel better. I suppose that affirms doing what your illness wants will only make it worse.

Upon arriving home I decided what I wanted to do with the night. Knowing anxiety awaited, I chose my ideal ending. I took a shower, then curled up on the couch with the iPad and raspberry chocolate fudge. Hot showers and baths are efficient anxiety relievers for me.

If there is one thing mental illness has taught me, it's that I need to make time for myself. Rushing through this world is not worth it. I want to be successful, but I want to enjoy my life more. I'm okay with taking the slow path to success if it means I can be happy for the journey.

Writing this now, my anxiety is welling up in my chest. I am apprehensive about tomorrow's therapy session. I am usually excited about therapy, but I do not know what she will say tomorrow. Having OCD, sometimes I feel a desperate need to either push for certainty or avoid altogether. Sometimes I can override that need and decide I do *not* want to push because knowing would only make me more anxious. Tomorrow, I do not want to know if that person called back. I do not want to ride that wave of anxiety I will get as she tells me the details of the call. Because of my OCD I often find that I do or do not wish to do something that an average person may do or not do easily. Knowing it is the OCD stopping me from living life how I should, I must bring myself to do that thing – or not do that thing as the case may be. I must tell OCD that it cannot control my life again. Based on what I've been through, I know I am strong. I've done things I never thought I could do since beginning treatment.

Therefore, I will end my day remembering all the times I did *not* give in to anxiety. I will remember each and every time I have taken a risk to get to where I am now. *Happy*.

You can follow Katlyn on Twitter @thekatway and her video blog, ShalomAleichem{Mental Health Vlogs}

A Day in My Head

Name: Cindy C
Age: 44
Condition: Borderline Personality Disorder
Location: Morinville, Central Alberta, Canada

After many years of being diagnosed with various forms of depression and anxiety issues, I have recently been diagnosed with GAD, (Generalized Anxiety Disorder), BPD (Borderline Personality Disorder) and MDD (Major Depressive Disorder).

I remember when my Psychiatrist first mentioned the Borderline Personality Disorder thing, I felt like my world was at an end. That I would never be the same person I was ever again. But after doing some research, I see that it is perhaps not as bad as I thought. That there may actually be some hope.

The depression and anxiety that have been a part of my life for a number of years weren't such bad things, since I was pretty much used to both already. And now that I've done some research into BPD, I do have at least some rays of light. That this isn't the end after all, like I originally thought.

Thanks for reading.

Name: David Stocks
Age: 50
Condition: Bipolar Disorder
Location: Staffordshire, United Kingdom
Profession: *Expert by Experience* for Dudley and Walsall Mental Health Partnership Trust

I started my day in my usual way with a cafetière of coffee in bed; I am not a morning person, so this helps kickstart my day. I am in fact a real coffee lover and often joke that I once got a job in a well-known coffee shop just to feed my caffeine addiction. From the moment I wake up my brain is on the go, fizzing with ideas and plans for the day. This is part of my bipolar, as I like to be slightly on the high side of my condition, in which my mood can swing dramatically up or down. I was asked recently to use one word to describe myself and I immediately replied "creative." My creativity seeps through into everything I do, today being no exception. Throughout my life I have found it difficult to control my creative mind, for I have great difficulty sticking to one task, with new ideas popping into my head all the time. This wandering mind, as I call it, means that I will often get side-tracked onto a different project, before completing the task in hand. This means my life has been littered with incomplete projects, and that I always have many things on the go at once. It is only really the last few years that I have begun to understand my wandering mind and made real progress in completing projects.

Whilst my mind was still spinning with ideas for the day, I eventually roused myself from my bed. As is usual for me, I had not left enough time to get washed and ready for my first task, a trust induction. I work as an Expert by Experience (EBE) for Dudley and Walsall Mental Health Partnership NHS Trust. I always joke that I have to be an expert in something. One of our roles as EBE is talking about our experience as mental health service users to new staff, or, in this case, student nurses.

Leaving a trail of domestic devastation behind me, which my wife Jules kindly puts back in order, I dash out to Bloxwich hospital where I am to deliver the training. I arrived a minute late, which is pretty good going for me, and joined my colleague Pat in the training room. Pat and I talked about our experiences as mental health service users. Pat is great, talking very openly and helping others. We have been nicknamed the dream team because of how well we work together. Though we are not the only dream team; *all* the Trust EBEs work well together, contributing in amazing ways to help improve the Trust's services and the lives of those who use them.

I talked about how it was a fellow service user who made me a cup of tea when I was first admitted to the acute ward in the middle of the night which ultimately led to a chain of events that changed my life and those around me forever. I won't go into details of this story, but key elements of it were my being featured in the Guardian next to Boris Johnson, with me wearing a mad hatters outfit (another story), and speaking in parliament and running a leadership programme for disabled people for four years. From that first cup of tea I have gone on to learn the true value of peer support, helping other people with similar experiences to myself, and more importantly, believing in each other. If it hadn't been for that cup of tea, I probably wouldn't be writing this now.

After the nurse induction I came home and painted a gate I had just made with wood preservative. Woodwork is one of my passions and an outlet for my creativity. The main part of the gate was made from interlocking walnut wood boards joined in free flowing curved patterns, with the top featuring a carved reindeer head, complete with antlers that are framed by an arch. The preservative brought out the richness of the walnut wood, whilst protecting it from the weather. It gave me a great feeling of satisfaction to see my completed project.

The highlight of my day though was the walk with our dog Storm. This is what I always look forward to most. Our walk takes us right out into nature, where Storm gets to run freely, chasing his ball, whilst we walk and enjoy the beauty all around us. I also take my camera, and was lucky enough this time to capture two herons and a little egret in flight together, truly magnificent birds.

Name: Shona Daly
Age: 39
Condition: Depression, Anxiety and Recovered Bulimic
Location: Norfolk, United Kingdom

How can this feel so surreal at the same time as feeling more real than anything ever before? Loaded up on fear, I closed my eyes and took the leap. I don't care anymore, yet I have never cared so much. I'm a girl of dichotomous extremes, I know that well. I'm fluorescent or I'm faded. I'm jumping or I'm lying down. I'm dancing or I'm crying. Today, the fear flooded in. It started getting a hold of my throat, I could feel it smothering my mind and my heart, and at the point where I would usually surrender to it, the point where it would usually have me shut down and sobbing, I faced up to the biggest fear of them all; I stood up to mental illness. I don't want this *thing* to be controlling me anymore, it has been for too long. I need to take back the control now and it has taken me this long to realize that I can. I've got this. I'm capable.

It's scarier than letting it hold you - there's a comfort in the familiarity of pathology and habit – but to take it into your own grasp and push it away from in front of your face, to not let its grip get onto you, that takes balls. And, I think maybe I just found mine. Gritting my teeth, I trusted myself and took charge. And you know what? I was OK. Because I don't want to feel like this anymore; this yearning to feel better, overwhelmed the feeling of stagnation. Like the final push in an arm wrestle, I found my force. I'm not taking this shit today. This shit has had me sodden with sadness, this shit has had me anchored in a state of anxiety and floored by self loathing for the whole of my life. This shit has had me starving my body for years, bent over a toilet with bloodied knuckles rammed down my throat more times than my heart wants to remember. But, this shit has brought me to now. It's got me to today. It is exactly what gave me the reckless determination to find the strength to smack it down, to be much stronger than it. This won't be conquered every time. I'm not so naive to think that. It will overpower me again, numerous times, it will tell me it's my ally, that it knows me best, and over and over again it will have me down on my knees and powerless. But today I fought back. Now I know I can. Now there's a strike on my side of the chalk board. Game. On.

Name: Tusilla Spring
Age: 52
Condition: Complex Post Traumatic Stress Disorder
Location: Helsinki, Finland

Many, many years ago, maybe almost a lifetime, something important occurred in my mind. Now, I would like to share this experience with you.

I was in a dark place. I can't remember where this particular darkness came from, it was just one of those numberless and blackened periods in which I came to the conclusion that I did not fit in. *Anywhere*.

I guess we all find ourselves in such places from time to time; some of us rarely, some of us
almost always.

The feeling might be familiar to you, the desperation of trying, the overwhelming sadness in failing, the envy of those who seem to succeed so effortlessly. They who succeed in society, in making friends, in establishing families, in being happy.

During my worst days, I frequently wanted to smash into tiny pieces the screen of my television set because the female program host was just so pretty and looked so self-assured. I didn't do it; after all, the TV was the only distraction tool I owned, and I had no money to buy a new one. I was also, of course, far too afraid to unleash my rage.

What happens when frustrations and disappointments load up over years, when there seems to be nobody in particular to blame, when it all boils down to the following line you spin yourself: "It's my fault, I'm useless, I'm worth nothing, I will always be a failure."

I was in this state for a long period. I was choking in my bitterness. I was crawling in my misery, thinking I'd just as well drown myself in it. My self-hatred knew no limits.

Then it happened: I suddenly became aware of a little girl standing in a corner. Her eyes were wide open in fear. She was hardly breathing. It seemed so much like she was trying to hide inside the wall, the way she pushed her tiny back against it. I could feel that she feared for her life. I could sense that I was the one that terrified her. And suddenly I realized that *she* was also a part of *me*.

Then, after some serious thinking, I confronted myself with the following realisation:

Yes, you are angry. Yes you are boiling over in frustration, and that I understand. However, you are not alone in there. Inside of you there is also a little girl. This little girl just wants to be a little girl. She wants to feel safe and appreciated. Right now, the little girl really wishes to paint and draw on a sheet of paper, and you will allow her to. You will organize for her a work station at the table, you will get bowls of water and sheets of paper and paint and brushes for her. Then you will gently lift her up and place her on the chair, wiping the tears off her face, saying sorry, I'm so sorry I frightened you that badly. I will make us cocoa and something to eat, and then I'll join you at the table.

And so I did. Not at once though, I had to go some more rounds with myself first. But eventually I gave in, concluding that to be in this state of self-destructions does no good at all. If I expect somebody to come help me out of it, knocking on my door, offering me comfort and support, then let's face it - nobody will. In fact, I am the only person who knows what I'm going through now, and I am the only person that can deal with it.

It is perfectly fine being this mad, I am allowed to be as mad as I want to, whenever I want to. However, this does not mean that it is fair to blame the little girl inside. She has nothing to do with it. These are adult problems. And besides, who knows: maybe in the long run the little girl inside actually turns out to be the one that leads you out of this misery, to a happier place?

Name: Vanessa Martin
Age: 28
Condition: Depression
Location: Solihull, United Kingdom

I awoke at 4.47am. I hadn't slept well as I'd had something on my mind the night before. I'm no longer clear as to whether I process things "normally" or over think them as I've been dealing with my mental health issues, specifically depression, for so long. The black dog that seems to be forever watching over me.

I managed to drift off back to sleep and awake again at the sound of my alarm, I hit snooze more times than I should have as I still fight the urge to stay in bed forever, but I eventually dragged my body out of my warm cocoon.

My morning at work was fairly average. I went into town at lunchtime and there was a choir congregated in the centre. I'd normally walk by, but I've been feeling extremely reflective recently following a huge dip in my mental health at the beginning of the year and fighting back from the brink of being suicidal, so I stopped to listen. Their harmonies were beautiful and I actually began to feel quite emotional. After feeling devoid of any real emotion other than bleakness for such a period, it's nice to have feelings again and connect to real things, so I try and take time to stop and appreciate the little things that passed me by in life prior to my breakdown.

When I got home I misplaced my phone. This happens often, but today I couldn't find it after searching seemingly everywhere. I went from being annoyed to mild rage in a heartbeat. I sat down and thought I'd look later, but I couldn't settle, as I felt anxious knowing I couldn't contact anyone. It feels like a safety net to me. It broke once, when I was extremely depressed, and an almighty panic attack ensued. I began searching like a crazed woman, looking in places such as the fridge, which I knew logically it wouldn't be in. I don't like that I get so worked up about such trivial things. At the back of my rational mind, I knew it would be in the house, but there was a pit of worry whirring in my stomach that wouldn't settle until I found it. Of course, it turned up in a shopping bag after about thirty minutes of frantic searching.

I decided to spend the evening trying to relax. Whenever I have free time I am guilty of letting my thoughts get away from me. What was once a small worry can become all-consuming in my mind, and today I had something bothering me. Nothing huge or even consequential but the quandary of something small festering in the back of my mind, so I needed to try and take my mind off it. I ran a bath and continued reading John Niven's "The Amateurs". I find reading is an incredibly helpful distraction from my own mind as I can submerge myself into the story of someone else's life.

I went to bed feeling quite content. Today had been a good day. I hadn't felt sad all day, and I was pleased that I had found time to enjoy things for myself, something that when I'm ill I often don't do. I was extremely tired following my night of disturbed sleep, so knew sleep wouldn't be far away, though did wonder for how long it would allow.

A Day in My Head

I'm relatively well at the moment, but depression can seem at times like a constant battle. A normal, apparently positive day can go flip in an instance, and fighting negative thoughts is challenging. But today, today was good.

Afterword

Name: Aron Bennett
Age: 30
Location: Norwich, United Kingdom

So here I am, back in Waterstones and having perused the books in the Biography section, I decide to partake in a quick refreshment in the reasonably priced in-store cafeteria. A woman behind me is conceitedly drinking a Lotus Biscoff Frappe while I sip on mango flavoured coconut water. On my table there is an old Fentimans ginger beer bottle with a flower in it, atop a stack of small books with titles such as *An Old Man's Love,* by Anthony Trollope. It's very artistic. I used to come here all the time with my laptop to write. I used to love writing. Now it's just the *idea* of writing that I love. Sertraline quells my anxiety, which in turn quells my creative flow. According to Martin Amis, still my favourite writer, "the writer's life is half ambition, half anxiety".

In fact, it was also Martin Amis who spoke, in a recent interview, of what he described as 'species consciousness'. The moral crash, particularly in the spirit of man post-September 11th, together with this great 'experiment in violence', in so many ways creating nothing so alienating, so utterly anomic to a new postmodern era. Wouldn't it be alluring or enamouring, even, such as the attempts to fix the anthropomorphic *egg* of old English nursery rhyme, to put the pieces all back together again ...

Despite a somewhat effete impulse to write, thankfully, *reading* is still on the cards for me and still provides a great deal of pleasure. It is a distraction away from my own problems and onto other people's which, without meaning in any way to sound perverse, seems always to help foster, at the very least, greater perspective. In fact, at its most glorious and effectual, reading has had a profoundly recuperative effect on my mental well-being, second only to the combined effects of Sertraline and exercise. To understand how others are feeling, whether they have a practical or even a positive message to impart or not, is strangely empowering. It makes us sit up. It provides us with a sense of long-awaited 'species consciousness'.

And hence the germ - an idea to collect stories on mental illness. It was during Christmas of 2015 and I just could not get this new scheme out of my head. Having met so many people living with mental illness from around the world, I knew there would be no scarcity in contributors. Unfortunately, I was also simultaneously met with the sad reality of the

A Day in My Head

publishing world; a world in which only famous people get to offload so prosperously and publicly. It didn't quite seem fair. Or, for that matter, conducive. And yet, commercially, these publishers had a gnat's whisker of a point – who amongst the 'ordinary' population would want to hear about the everyday lives of complete and utter strangers ...

And that's where the idea of a *diary* became galvanised. A day in which close to one hundred experiences, some ordinary some ultra-mundane, might be shared pithily, though heartily, and with candour, from around the entire globe. Surely that would have the desired impact? Surely that would be interesting enough for a voracious readership so used to hearing about *Jordan's* next breast augmentation or the bedroom 'goings on' of an ex *Essex Wives* 'celebrity'?

And so I gathered up contributors via any and every means possible. Like a squirrel on steroids, I collected volunteer after volunteer. And the more I collected, the more golden nuggets and pearly words of true wisdom gleaned, the more I became enthralled. I became positively addicted to meeting new and interesting people with stories to tell, many of which resonating not only deeply with me but with the content of so much other stuff I had the privilege to now be reading.

Species consciousness – I had found it in abundance.

Late on in April – and whilst still recruiting for people to write – I decided I wanted to get in touch with a woman and writer who has remained perhaps my biggest influence to date: Sally Brampton. If anybody encapsulated Amis' *'ambition, anxiety'* paradigm then it was her. Ex-editor of *Elle* Magazine and the author of one of the most beautifully written memoirs of depression ever written - *Shoot the Damn Dog* - Sally was perhaps *the* reason why I ever turned to writing in the first place.

And so a few weeks later, I put a search into Twitter: S-A-L-L-Y B-R-A-M-P-T-O-N. It came just after I had recruited a well-known MP, and just before bagging me a bit-actress from *Game of Thrones*. Though instead of her profile, the first result was a tweet, two tweets, three tweets, a myriad of tweets *about* her. They were messages of heartfelt condolences. An online Guardian report posted not long before my search revealed that she had died. It seemed somehow unthinkable. Apparently, she had simply just walked out into the water, like Virginia Woolf and Ophelia before her, and ended her life. After years of campaigning and a long, punishing period resulting in a gradual recovery, the black dog had finally sunk its canine teeth in for the last time. And for the first time ever, I wanted to mourn for somebody I had never even met.

That evening I wrote the following on Facebook:

I don't usually do this but really sad story in the news just a few hours ago. Sally Brampton, journalist, writer and mental health campaigner died today at aged 60.

Her Book 'Shoot The Damn Dog', a memoir chronicling her severe depression, is what got me into writing in the first place and opened my eyes up to the intense meaning and structure that writing brings. The psychiatrist Victor Frankl posited that the main search of mankind is not happiness or pleasure, but meaning. "Life is never made unbearable by circumstances, but only by lack of meaning and purpose."

Through her honest and fluid writing style, Sally made a connection with her audiences and reached out and touched others suffering with mental illness. It was a book that avoided any possible accusation of self-gratification or gratuitous egoism and helped to end what is so commonly seen as one of the last taboos.

Today I went to email her, perhaps unconsciously prompted by mentions of her on Twitter, to see if she would be involved in a project involving one hundred plus people writing about their mental illnesses from around the world on May 16th. It seems a cruel twist that I should find that she died only a few hours earlier. . .

Sally gave a lot of people meaning and I hope our new book can achieve just half of that positive momentum.

Sharing stories, enhancing our collective understanding - I realised, perhaps only *after* I had embarked on the project, that the key to all of this, to ending stigma, to generating compassion and even to aiding recovery, to borrow again from Brampton, is *connection*. And so I will leave you with a few words, which for me, sums up everything I hope this project is all about. And I really hope, more than ever, it has been successful in those aims:

"We forget that others understand our suffering. We withdraw, isolate or shut down completely. We lose ourselves in our selves, and in the illness. It doesn't have to be that way. If we connect with even one other human being who truly understands, we take one step out of the illness. Life is about connection. There is nothing else."

CPSIA information can be obtained
at www.ICGtesting.com
Printed in the USA
BVOW04s0923281116

469019BV00007B/5/P